SQL and Other Important Database Topics

SQL and Other Important Database Topics

First Edition

Understanding relational databases, SQL and
how to access, manage and use data

Thomas E. Meers

GOM BIZPRESS
COLUMBUS, OHIO

GOM BIZPRESS
An Imprint of Gom Publishing
4801 Roberts Road, Suite P, Columbus, Ohio 43228

Phone: 866.466.2608
Email: communications@gompublishing.com

To Order: 800.231.6597
www.gompublishing.com

Second GomBizpress paperback printing: November 2003

Contents

Acknowledgements

I would like to thank the following people for their support, encouragement, and efforts in helping me produce this, my first, book which was a life goal for me:

My wife, Laura, who, aside from being a great spouse, has been an exceptional business partner in addition to providing me with the necessary companionship, love, and foundation for all of my accomplishments.

My brother, Dan, who has been a consistent encouragement and invaluable in helping me become an author. His undying support has been very much appreciated.

My friends and associates at Result Data in Columbus, Ohio, who have helped me learn and improve my understanding of all sorts of things. They are without at doubt the best team I have ever worked with.

My parents, who raised me to believe that I can do anything. A great way to approach an endeavor as demanding as this book has been on my time and attention.

Chapter 1:
Introduction

Some Background

I wrote this text as part of an effort to collect and make sense of a variety of topics that center on accessing, managing, and utilizing data from SQL databases. My background as a systems engineer and programmer has provided me with, what I believe to be, a fairly comprehensive view of database technology and how it has been used over the span of the microcomputer industry's history. It was well over 20 years ago when my first experience with databases began on an Apple II computer. The databases software was a product called VisiFile. I remember exploring the incomplete documentation and experimenting with various concepts in the basement of parents' house. While I never fully comprehended that software, it launched me on a journey of interest in how information might be accumulated, stored, and shared. It also—and more importantly—opened my mind to the idea that if information is stored in a predetermined manner the ability to use it to answer questions would be nothing short of revolutionary.

After several years of college and some rudimentary courses on computers and programming, I began working with the then state of the art computer systems in the UNIX world. This was before PC's and networks had become accepted in the work place. The technology that I was reared on included AT&T and Fortune Systems Unix. While my role was in the project management and business side of things at the time I again encountered database technology and was intrigued. This compelled me to become more technically oriented, and I found that my skills and interest in the technical side were fairly strong despite my distaste for math in high school. My career took a turn towards the technical side of the then young and wild industry. As a UNIX/network engineer, my skills and knowledge progressed, and the advent of the PC and local area network passed. I discovered that my fellow engineers were very reluctant to work with software applications. They wanted to focus on the wiring, electronics, and hardware associated with connecting computers together. Their reluctance, and in some cases fear, of taking responsibility for software concerned me. My disposition and view of the industry had started with the idea of managing data, and I saw network engineering as no more than a means to an end. This short-sightedness on my colleagues' behalf encouraged me to become a programmer. I saw this as a competitive advantage in a very "dog eat dog" industry. After all, it was the "eighties."

Becoming a "programmer" in the microcomputer world was a very informal thing in those days. One simply started programming by obtaining a compiler program and reading reference manuals and books. There was no Internet at the time and online services, bulletin boards and the like were unorganized and difficult to use. Getting sample code, other examples and assistance was difficult. One of the first problems that I encountered was centered on how to store information. Most programming languages only offered the ability to write files to disk which worked well enough for a single users, but created serious issues for an audience of more than one person. Problems concerning file and record locking were common. Some languages like dBase, Paradox and DataFlex had database capabilities build in, which went a long way to solving this problem. However, for the most part, database languages used sequential data storage. This meant that the programmer had a lot of work to do in order to produce even simple presentations of the data on the screen or in printed form. I remember spending significant effort and time creating data grids so the user could scroll up and down as she browsed records. In the early days data storage was "record" based, which means one had to manage every aspect of presentation.

Eventually, Relational Database Management Systems (RDBMS) with early versions of Structure Query Language (SQL) emerged. This changed the way programmers and other technical people dealt with data by providing the ability to work with sets of data. The common term of the day was "Client/Server." This approach has become the *de facto* standard for how most software systems store and access data. Database systems from companies like Oracle, IBM, and Microsoft follow this model, and industry standards for SQL and RDBMS have been established to which most manufacturers adhere.

This book is my effort to present the relevant information necessary to access, manage, and maintain SQL databases. I offer this information in the most generic manner possible and have endeavored not to lean towards any manufacturer's specific enhancements. The information in this book should apply to most leading databases including those from Oracle, Microsoft, IBM, and others. I have also attempted to include the necessary background topics regarding database connectivity to assure that those who are new to the topic have a comprehensive view of the overall client/server model. While new technologies are emerging at an unprecedented rate, most of them are dependant upon SQL-compliant databases. This includes Web and Business intelligence systems. For this reason the content of this book is valuable to Web developers, database administrators, and programmers of almost every type. However, if you are not a programmer, don't fret. The material is equally valuable to anyone who may need to access and understand databases and data.

Many of my company's consultants, associates, and customers use the SQL language in their day to day work. They use it with databases and software development tools. While most of them have exceptional SQL skills, I have found that even the most experienced individuals tend to have "blind spots" in areas of the language that they don't frequent. Additionally, many of our business intelligence specialist and customers don't write enough SQL on a regular basis to remain mindful of the requirements of the language. This text is designed to assist in the learning and use of SQL for all types of people. It is organized in a practical and logical manner. It is also filled with tips and examples to make short work of using and optimizing SQL syntax. However, this book also goes further. It is designed to address more fundamental issues concerning how client computers access SQL based systems. I hope that you find this book helpful not only as a SQL reference and tutorial also but as a book that helps you see the entire picture of client/server computing.

To get more information please visit www.resultdata.com and check the Bibliography of this text for recommended reading.

Document Conventions

Examples

Examples in this document will, in some cases, be forced to word-wrap making it difficult to determine where actual line feeds occur. In these cases there may be an underscore (_) character placed at the end of the line that is wrapping. This character is not part of the syntax and should be omitted when attempting to use the source code examples. This will not always be done since this text is available in e-book format in which case word wrapping will vary depending on the reader's screen settings and resolution.

SQL Syntax

SQL sample syntax will appear in a fixed space font to make it easier to understand. It will also have SQL key words highlighted in bold text.

Where appropriate special attention has be given to laying out the syntax to make it easy to follow. This is an example:

```
SELECT
        organization_name,
        city
FROM
        tb_account
```

SQL Results

Results from a SQL statement that returns data (not all of them do) will sometimes be referred to as a "result set," "data set," "record set," or "row set". All of these terms mean the same thing. SQL results will appear in a fixed space font to make it easy to understand them. This is an example:

```
organization_name                          city
-------------------------------------------------
Energy Source Diet Centers                 Piedmont
Lee Stairworks and Carpentry, Inc.         Key West
Nirabi Auto Service                        Detroit
Air Barbados                               Lake Forest
```

Column Naming

It is important to note that column names in SQL Statements can often be prefixed with the corresponding table names. While this is not always necessary, it can be done at any time. This text will combine these approaches. The following examples are equivalent:

```
tb_account.acount_name
account_name
```

Chapter 2:
Understanding Databases

This chapter provides a general background on databases and database server technology to help you understand how SQL systems work and how various software packages and web sites can connect to SQL data and utilize it.

Database Servers

Relational Database Management Systems (RDBMS) implement, in most cases, what is known as the "Client-Server" systems model. This means that users of the database typically run some sort of software on their computers (the Client) that interact with the server which has the appropriate database software installed on it (i.e. MS-SQL Server, Oracle, or DB2). In order for the client computer to access the server, it must be connected to the network, and it must, among other things, have the appropriate database client software installed. Figure 2-1 illustrates the necessary elements that are used to create a client-server connection.

Figure 2-1 an example of the Client-Server model

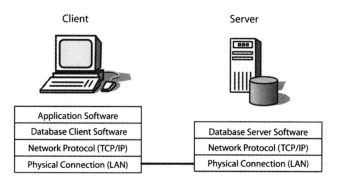

With increasing popularity software applications are being written to take advantage of web servers for Internet, Intranet, and Extranet applications. These applications still need access to data from SQL compliant databases. However, in these cases the client is the Web server, and the actual end user is viewing, exporting, and printing data as a Web client rather than a database client. Figure 2-2 illustrates the use of a Web server as a database client.

Figure 2-2: The use of a Web Server to Distribute Client-Server data

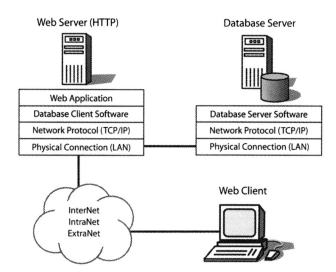

Database client software is a requirement for enabling any computer, a client PC or a web server, to communicate with a database server. Without client software the applications that are installed on a computer or Web server can not communicate with the corresponding database. All database manufacturers include client software for distribution to client PC's and Web servers. Their respective licensing requirements for the use of the client software vary. In some cases the client software may be included with other software. For example, Microsoft has included core elements of its SQL Server database client in recent versions of Microsoft Windows and its data access components (MDAC) for older versions of Windows. The following represent examples of database client software for some of the more popular databases:

- MS-SQL Server Client Utilities
- The Oracle Client
- Client Access for the IBM AS/400
- The IBM DB2 Client

Data Connectivity Enhancements (ODBC & ADO)

The Open Database Connectivity (ODBC) standard was created by Microsoft to standardize the way in which application software accesses databases. It has been a part of the Microsoft Windows operating system for almost a decade. The idea behind it is to add an additional layer of translation to the Client-Server model so that programmers can design their software in a way that doesn't require them to recode if the underlying database type changes. For example, if a programmer writes an application specifically for an Oracle database and then if his users decide they want to switch to IBM DB2, the program will have to be modified to accommodate the change. If the programmer writes the program to use ODBC, this change can occur without requiring the programmer to revisit the underlying source code. ODBC has not always fulfilled on its promise of database independence for programmers. Its many versions and software drivers have sometimes been an issue. However, many database manufacturers have adopted this standard as a means to provide access to their database software products. In many cases ODBC does resolve a variety of database connectivity problems and is considered common place in most corporate and government production environments. The illustration in figure 2-3 shows how ODBC inserts itself in the Client-Server model.

ActiveX Data Object (ADO) and Object Linking & Embedding Database (OLEDB) are the next generation of database connectivity by Microsoft. They offer better and faster connectivity by embracing the database manufacturers and allowing them to optimize their use of the new standard. OLEDB include backwards compatibility to the older ODBC standard, and ODBC continues to be very popular with older as well as new software applications. It's important to understand that ODBC and ADO/OLEDB do not replace the database client software. These interfaces add an extra layer to the model but provide a more generic way for application software to access databases. Most popular software programs like Microsoft Access and Crystal Reports can use these mechanisms to access data from a variety of database systems. In some cases ODBC is the only method available for accessing certain types of data.

Figure 2-3 How ODBC and OLEDB help in database connections

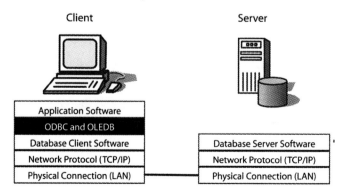

Relational Database Concepts

Originally, computer data was stored sequentially. That means that the pieces of data (each character or digit, sometimes referred to as a byte) were stored in a predefined order. To produce a list of items from the data, a programmer would read some of the data into memory from the disk or tape where it was stored and then parse the sequence of elements. The positions of the elements were predefined and allocated in a sequence. To get data out of such a sequence, usually stored as a sequential file, you would have to be a programmer or have a program written with a very specific purpose in mind. All types of data retrieval under this model were tedious especially the development of printed reports. Figure 2-4 illustrates how sequential data might be organized.

Figure 2-4 An illustration of sequential data

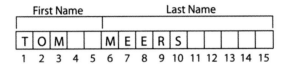

The illustration in figure 2-4 shows how sequential storage works. Each aspect of data is stored in a given position. In this example the "first name" field has positions 1 through 5 allocated, and the "last name" field has positions 6 through 15 allocated. Among other things this type of storage requires the programmer to handle data types like integers or floating point numbers in a defined way. It is a simple, but limited, method for storing information and requires extensive effort from software developers (programmers).

Relational databases offer a more planned and structured approach to storing data. SQL offers a universal language for managing and retrieving the data. In a relational database the data is broken out by category into what are called tables. A table is conceptually similar to a ledger or worksheet where there are columns across the top and rows down the side. Each row then represents a "record" of data where the columns define the various sub-categories or "fields" for each record. The number of columns is usually limited while the number of rows (records) can increase to very large numbers.

Each table represents a specific topic like "customer data" or "order data." These tables can then be related to each other to produce sets of data that meet specific needs. Additionally, relational databases offer the ability to enforce certain rules that assure that the data is properly maintained. For example, if we remove a customer from the Customers table, what happens to the corresponding orders for that customer that are stored in the Orders table? The database system can be designed to automatically remove the associated orders from the Orders table. This is known as Referential Integrity (RI). Referential integrity provides a means for maintaining a certain consistency in the data between tables. It is not always used since similar abilities can be offered by the software applications that use the database. However, referential integrity offers a uniform way of enforcing constraints on the data. This is of particular importance when a database is to be shared by several software applications and may receive new data or updates from more than one of them.

It's important to understand that a defined relationship between tables is not required in order to join the tables to get a combined data set back. The purpose of the relationship is to enable and enforce referential integrity. Although relationships aren't necessary to join tables together in a SQL statement, they do act as a good indicator for how to join tables. Figure 2-5 shows an Entity Relationship (ER) diagram illustrating how two tables might be related to each other. The diagram shows the table names and the columns for each table in a standardized notation. This is a typical example of what is commonly referred to as a data model.

In figure 2-5 the tb_account and tb_order tables have a defined relationship based on the account_id column. This relationship is based on indexes called keys. An index is a mechanism that the database uses to make the sorting and searching for data more efficient. Indexes and

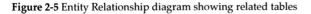

Figure 2-5 Entity Relationship diagram showing related tables

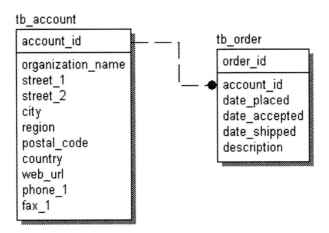

keys can be created using SQL. The Primary Key (PK) in the diagram is associated with the Accounts table. A primary key must represent a unique value or combination of values for every row allowed in the table. The Foreign Key (FK) on the Orders table does not enforce uniqueness, but represents an index on the column to which the data from the first table (Accounts) relates. By having an index on the AccountID columns of both tables, a relationship can be established between the tables. This relationship allows the creation and enforcement of referential integrity which can force data in the second table (Orders) to automatically change upon revisions to the first table (Accounts). Referential integrity reduces the effort required by application programmers and assures that data will be consistent between the two tables without concern for which software application is used to add or update the data.

Chapter 3:
SQL History & Fundamentals

This chapter offers a short history of SQL and a breakdown of the basic SQL data types and special characters that are fundamental to its use. This information will help you begin to understand why SQL exists and how basic SQL statements are constructed.

The History of SQL

SQL was originally created by IBM Corporation to improve and ease the retrieval of data from, and interaction with, databases. It was created as part of an ongoing effort to define standards for a relational model of database management that was started by Dr. E. F. Codd at the IBM Research Laboratory in San Jose, California. As SQL evolved other vendors like Oracle Corporation and Microsoft began to adopt and influence it. In 1992 a relatively complete standard for SQL was published by the American National Standards Institute (ANSI) and International Standards Organization (ISO). This standard is often referred to as the ANSI-92, or the SQL2, standard. Later, in 1999, ANSI published the

ANSI-99, or SQL3, standard, which enhanced the ANSI-92 standard. At the time of the writing of this text, the ANSI-99 (SQL3) standard has become relatively common for the latest release of database software from many leading database manufacturers including Oracle, Microsoft, and others. While, in most cases, these manufactures also have maintained compatibility with most aspects of the older ANSI-92 standard it is clear that the intention is to move toward the newer standard. Where appropriate this text will show the syntax for both standards, but the emphasis will be on the more modern SQL3 standard. The time line in figure 3-1 illustrates the approximate dates for each major revision of the SQL standards.

Figure 3-1 SQL Standards and release dates

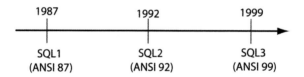

SQL Basics

SQL is recognized as the *de facto* standard for communicating with most database systems. It is accepted and endorsed by virtually all database manufacturers, software companies, and developers. The use of SQL and the dependency of many organizations on it are growing at a rapid rate. Knowing SQL and how to use it is considered by many to be a prerequisite for programming, report design, database administration, and business analyst positions. SQL provides an "English like" manner for interacting with databases. Its name, "Structured Query Language," is somewhat misleading in that SQL provides facilities for managing data structures, updating, and managing data as well as "querying" or retrieving data. The current standard for SQL is broken out into three primary categories:

- **Data Definition**—This includes the ability to establish and maintain data structures (tables, columns, etc.). These structures represent the way in which the data is organized and stored to make retrieval effective and efficient. The parts of SQL that handle this are referred to as Data Definition Language (DDL).

- **Data Management**—This represents the actual creation, manipulation, and retrieval of the data itself (rows). The parts of SQL that handle this are referred to as Data Management Language (DML) and include operations like inserting, updating, and deleting rows of data.

- **Data Control**—This manages the way in which data is accessed. It includes the management of security and user rights and restrictions. It also includes features that provide recovery capabilities in the event of a system failure. The parts of SQL that handle this are referred to as Data Control Language (DCL).

SQL also facilitates various capabilities that allow a database structure to adhere to the standards for Relational Database Management Systems (RDBMS). This includes the abilities to define functional relationships between tables of data. These relationships help to assure that data is maintained in a consistent and meaningful way. This feature set is called Referential Integrity and, while not always implemented, gives the database designer the ability to enforce rules on the creation and manipulation of data so that it is accurate and consistent across various categories (tables).

SQL Data Types

Database columns must store data in a predefined data manner. This is sometimes called "data typing." The data type of each column determines how the data in a column can be manipulated. For example, numeric values can be summed, but character values—like names and words—can not. The following is a short list of the more common data types used in most popular databases:

- **CHAR, TEXT, or STRING** (alphanumeric characters in fixed length)
- **VARCHAR** (like Char, but variable length) *n VCHAR*
- **INTEGER** (whole numbers only) *no decimals*
- **CURRENCY or MONEY** (floating point numbers with 4 decimal places)
- **DOUBLE or FLOAT** (floating point number with x decimal places) *as many decimal places as needed*
- **DATETIME** (combination of date & time—will hold just date)
- **BOOLEAN or BIT** (a true/false value)

0 = False
1 = True (sometimes) *-1 = True*

Null Values

A column in a SQL database table can be configured so that data is not required in order for a row to be inserted or updated. That is to say, some columns in a row may be left empty. This means that when a row is inserted into the table, if no value is assigned to a given column, the column will have a value of NULL (or nothing). Null is not the same as zero nor is it the same as a zero length string (for example, the value between double quotes). Null is a separate and unique value (or, more correctly, lack of value) that may or may not be allowed in a given column. It represents that idea that no value was ever assigned to a row-column combination or that a previous value was removed as opposed to reset or changed. The following list will help you understand the concept of Null a little better:

- NULL values can be evaluated in a SQL statement.
- NULL values are not the same as a Zero (0) or empty strings (zero length string).
- Some Columns will be configured not to allow NULLs (requiring a value in order for a record to be added or updated).

Wildcards, Constants & Special Characters

When you are selecting data in a SQL statement, you can use various characters to control which data is returned. These items are part of the SQL syntax requirements and thus are considered reserved words. That means that these characters, when used in certain ways, will have special meaning to the database server and result in specific actions that are taken by the server. You may need to use wildcard or special characters that have predefined meanings in the SQL syntax to accomplish certain things. SQL syntax is similar to most programming languages in that it has several types of reserved words and characters. They include wildcard characters, constant or literal values, and key words that represent commands.

Wildcards are special characters that can be used to represent certain matching characteristics. For example, if you wanted all of something, you might use the asterisk (*). Constants are words or characters that you type into your SQL statement to specify a match on some known and static value. Constants must be represented as a specific data type (i.e., numeric, character, Boolean, date/time).

Here are some basics on wildcards and constants:

* (Asterisk)

The asterisk indicates a selection of "all." It is commonly used to select all columns in a table.

% (Percent Sign)

The percent sign is used to select "any" character in a given position. For example this wildcard is sometimes used with the LIKE operator to return all values that begin with or contain certain characters.

" (Double Quote)

The double quote characters are sometimes used to reference table or columns names that have more than one word (names with spaces in them). These are called **quoted identifiers** and they may vary from one manufacturer to another. Sometimes the [bracket] characters are used for this purpose as well.

' (Single Quote)

The single quote characters are used to represent a character or date/time constant value. A number enclosed in single quotes will be interpreted as a character data type. If the characters are in date/time format and compared to a date/time field, the values will be interpreted as date/time.

-- (Two Dashes)

Two dashes mean that the text that follows is a comment and will not be interpreted as part of the SQL statement.

/* (Forward Slash + Asterisk)

The forward slash followed by an asterisk demarks that beginning of a comment block. Reversing the characters (*/) demarks the end of a comment block. This allows you to add long comments to your SQL statement without having to begin each line with two dashes.

Chapter 4:
Beginning to Access Data

This chapter covers a variety of topics that pertain to the way in which we retrieve information from an SQL compliant database. The main SQL command for doing this is the SELECT command. However, there are a variety of methods and options that affect how the SELECT command operates. The SELECT command allows you to retrieve a specific set of data from the database server. It is the most popular command in the SQL language because the most common interaction with databases is based on retrieving data. This chapter will address the most common and relevant approaches.

Simple SELECT Statement Syntax

```
SELECT
   ColumnName, ColumnName...
FROM
   TableName
ORDER BY
   TableName.ColumnName [Asc, Desc]
```

Basic Selection (retrieval) of Data

The SELECT command provides a way to retrieve specified data from one or more tables or views in a SQL database. This is the most common type of SQL statement and can be used in conjunction with other SQL commands to provide very specific results. The basic elements of the SELECT command include the ability to determine which columns you want returned. A SELECT statement will return a data set (a list of rows for the selected columns).

The following is simple example of a SELECT statement that returns the organization name, city, and phone number from a table called tb_accounts. In this example the SELECT statement is designed to return only a few columns of data from the accounts table. If the list of columns (separated by commas) were to be replaced with the asterisk character (*), all columns from the accounts table would be returned.

```
SELECT
    organization_name,
    city,
    phone_1
FROM
    tb_account
```

This statement will return a record set that looks similar to the following:

```
organization_name                      city        phone_1
--------------------------------------------------------------
Energy Source Diet Centers             Piedmont    1632011093
Lee Stairworks and Carpentry, Inc. Key West        5727712780
Nirabi Auto Service                    Detroit     8693149323
Air Barbados                           Lake Forest 1439110024
```

Eliminating Duplicate Records

Sometimes, there is more than one record with the same information (the same column values) returned by a SELECT statement. While, in some cases, this may be desirable, sometimes you will want such duplicate rows eliminated so that you only get one row for each row that is duplicated. To deal with this you can add the keyword DISTINCT to your SELECT statement so that duplicate rows are eliminated from your result set. It's important to note that the DISTINCT keyword will operate on all of the columns that you include in your SELECT statement. For example, if you are using the asterisk to include all columns from a given table (SELECT *), the DISTINCT feature will only eliminate duplicates where all columns contain the same values in two or more records. The following is an example of a simple SELECT statement using DISTINCT. It shows how you can get a distinct list of cites from a table that would return duplicates otherwise.

```
SELECT DISTINCT
   city
FROM
   tb_account
```

Notice that the DISTINCT keyword appears right after the SELECT command. This helps to show that it applies to all of the following columns. If it were used with the asterisk wildcard, the column order would be whatever the database designer determined when the table was created or last altered.

Sorting Data (the ORDER BY clause)

Rows of data are normally returned in what is known as original order. This is the order in which the data was inserted into the database table over time. For example, if three data entry people added new records to the database at different times in the morning, their corresponding rows would be appended to the end of the table based on the order that they were saved. Most database systems handle deadlock situations—two or more records are inserted at the same time—in an automatic way. So a time oriented sequence will still dictate the order of the records in the table. This order, original order, is also known as natural order. Usually, original order is not desirable since it does not lend itself to effective use or review of the data. From a user's point of view original order appears to be random. To change the order of the results returned by a SELECT statement, you can add what is known as an ORDER BY clause. The ORDER BY clause will force the record set to be sorted in a predefined manner. The following shows the same SELECT statement from above where we wanted to get a distinct list of cities from the tb_accounts table. However, in this statement the cities will be listed in name order.

```
SELECT DISTINCT
    city
FROM
    tb_account
ORDER BY
    city
```

This statement will return a record set that looks similar to the following:

```
city
------------------------
Albuquerque
Anchorage
Andover
Aspen
Atlanta
Baltimore
Baton Rouge
Berkeley
Beverly Hills
```

The ORDER BY clause can also be used to sort the results of a SELECT statement in different orders: ascending or descending. This is done by adding the words "Asc" or "Desc" to the end of the ORDER BY clause.

These words stand for "Ascending" and "Descending," respectively. The default sort of an ORDER BY clause is ascending so, if there is no specific directive indicating sort order, ascending will be used. The following statement is the same as the last statement, but the sort order is descending order:

```
SELECT DISTINCT
    city
FROM
    tb_account
ORDER BY
    City DESC
```

This statement will return a record set that is sorted from Z to A, or in descending order, as shown below:

```
city
------------------------
Wheeling
Washington D.C.
Waikkiki
Vail
Urbana
Tucson
Topeka
```

Controlling Result Sets (WHERE)

A SELECT statement can return a very large number of rows. When a SELECT statement is executed against a database table with no filtering instructions, the database server performs what is called a table scan. This means that every row in the table is reviewed by the database server. Table scans are big problems for database servers and their administrators. SQL databases are engineered to work very well with smaller data sets. A SELECT statement that returns a few hundred or even a few thousand rows is usually not a problem. However, modern database tables may contain millions or even billions of rows. An attempt to retrieve this sort of row quantity creates serious performance issues and may even bring the database server down. Additionally, there is no practical reason for an application or user to ever want this much output from the database. It is simply too much information to serve any practical purpose.

To limit the amount of data accessed and returned by a SELECT statement, you can use the WHERE clause. It adds the ability to filter the result so that only the rows that match certain conditions are included. For example, you may wish to get a list of accounts, but you might want it limited to accounts that are located in the state of California. The follow SELECT statement and WHERE clause will filter out all non-California accounts while showing some basic accounting information.

```
SELECT DISTINCT
    tb_account.organization_name,
    tb_account.city,
    tb_account.phone_1
FROM
    tb_account
WHERE
    tb_account.region = 'CA'
ORDER BY
    organization_name ASC
```
→ not required

This statement will return results similar to the following. Notice that the order is based on the organization name due to the ORDER BY clause. The number of records in this statement is limited by the WHERE clause to only include accounts in 'CA.'

```
organization_name                       city          phone_1
-----------------------------------------------------------
Brand Y Creative Services               Oak Lawn      6493971348
Car Suite Cleaners                      San Francisco 1276322169
Elle Hypnosis and Therapy Center        San Diego     4141177805
Elm Place Business Supplies             Santa Barbara 8779033924
```

The WHERE clause employs the use of more than just a reserved word (WHERE). It also requires that you also use a constant value to perform data matching. This means that you must begin to take note of data types.

Notice in the preceding SELECT statement that the abbreviation for the state of California is surrounded by single quotes. This is how you pass a string (or character) data type as a constant value to the database server. You might also notice that this statement makes use of an "operator." The equals sign (=) tells the database server how to match the data. Notice in the next SELECT statement and in its results that we can change the operator to show all accounts that are not in the state of California. In this case we show a "less than" operator next to a "greater than" operator to tell the database server to find all accounts that do not have CA as a region.

```
SELECT DISTINCT
    tb_account.organization_name,
    tb_account.city,
    tb_account.phone_1
FROM
    tb_account
WHERE
    tb_account.region <> 'CA'
ORDER BY
    organization_name ASC
```
→ not required

This statement returns accounts that do not have CA as a region identifier.

organization_name	city	phone_1
AA Advertising	Shaumburg	2237417427
AAA Daniels Antiques	Bloomington	8077653120
Acturial Enterprises Ltd.	North Chicago	0703344502
Block Boats and Lures	Albequerque	1416238990
Chands CPA	Waukegan	4537132984
Cosmo Skin Care Center	Birmingham	4628780349
Cotton Thumb Ltd.	New Orleans	6425245992

The operators that can be used to match data include all of the standard operators found in most programming and macro languages. They typically will operate against most data types. Here is a short list of most common operators:

- $\geq$ = greater than equal to $\leq$ less than equal to
- = Equal To
- > Greater Than
- < Less Than
- != ; <> Not Equal To
- not → not (salary =10000) Salary <> 10000 Salary != 10000

doesn't work in oracle

These are covered in more detail in the next chapter.

Chapter 5:
More Sophisticated Data Retrieval

A basic SQL query that uses simple WHERE clause logic is adequate to get you started. However, it is inevitable that you will need to perform more complex searching for data. Relational databases (SQL databases) are engineered to allow you to get simple answers to complex questions. The more complex the question is the more direct and valuable the answer. For this reason it is very import to take a look at some of the more complex methods for controlling the results of a SQL query.

There are several things that you can do to enhance the control over what rows a SELECT statement will return. In the previous chapter you saw a simple evaluation using standard operators like equal, greater than, etc. In this chapter we'll take a look at several more advanced topics, including:

- More about Operators
- Using a Logical OR
- Intentional Mismatching (NOT)
- Compound WHERE Clause Logic
- Partial Matching (LIKE)

More about Operators

The WHERE clause acts as a filter to limit or reduce the number of rows (records) that the statement returns in the result set. As you saw in the previous chapter, special characters called "operators" help to facilitate this. Each operator has a specific purpose that allows you to determine if a column value matches a constant value or another column. The following is a description of the main operators in SQL:

= (Equal To) — Where values on both sides of the operator must match for rows to be included in the result set.

> (Greater Than) — Where the value on the left must be greater than the value on the right for rows to be included in the result set.

< (Less Than) — Where the value on the left must be less than the value on the right side in order for rows to be included in the result set.

<> (Not Equal To) — Where the data on both sides of the operator does not match. In this case all rows that do not have a match will be included in the result set.

These operators are sometimes referred to as "scalar" because they are used in scalar expressions for evaluation. The idea of something being scalar has to do with its affect on a quantity without regard for direction. These operators allow us to control the quantity of rows returned without consideration for a standard direction (i.e., greater, less, etc). We can control quantity in all directions. Combining operators can also be done to include exact matches when using > or < operators. When doing this the equals operator always comes last. This will return a result set that meets the > or < condition, but if a record is equal to the criterion, it will also be included. The following statement shows the combination of the "greater than" and "equals" operators:

```
SELECT
   organization_name,
   city,
   region
FROM
   tb_account
WHERE
   region >= 'O'
ORDER BY
   Region
```

It returns results where accounts are located in regions that begin with the letter "O" or a letter that comes after "O" in the alphabet. The results would look similar to the following:

```
organization_name              city                  region
----------------------------------------------------------
DBN Bank                       Bloomfield Hills      OH
Deer Lake Inn                  West Bloomfield Hills OK
MedicServe Medical Supply      Lahiana               OK
Metro Appliance Service        Tombsville            OR
Gourmet the Frog               Chelsea               PA
```

Notice that the regions only include those that begin with "O" or later letters. Also, if the equals sign had been removed, the regions would include those that begin with "P" or later.

The common operators can be used on all data types. They are not limited in this respect. For example, you can use the "equals" and "greater than" operators together on numeric columns and the mathematical value of the data and constant will determine the results. The following statement would return all products with a price of $50 or more:

```
SELECT
   product_name,
   unit_price
FROM
   tb_product
WHERE
   unit_price >= 50.00
```

Partial Matching (LIKE)

Sometimes the data that you want to retrieve will not have an exact match to the criteria that must be used to retrieve it. For example, it is possible that you are looking for all records that begin with or contain a certain word or phrase. To do this in SQL, you will need to use the LIKE method. LIKE allows you to perform partial matching by combining its syntax with wildcards. There are three basic applications of the LIKE method. They include performing matches on the basis of a column beginning with, ending with, or containing a certain set of characters. The LIKE method is a very powerful and, therefore, a very popular way to filter data in SQL statements.

Begins With

The LIKE method can be used to retrieve rows that match a character or string of characters like a word or phrase. A common use of the LIKE method involves retrieving the rows that begin with a word or phrase. To do this you use the LIKE keyword and place a wildcard character at the end of your criteria. To perform a "begins with" match, the wild card is placed at the end of the criteria to tell the server to ignore all characters after it. For example, to get all accounts where the company name begins with the letter "A," your SQL select statement would look like the following:

```
SELECT
    *
FROM
    tb_account
WHERE
    organization_name
LIKE 'A%'
```

Ends With

The LIKE method can also allow you to search for a match on a column where the value ends with a certain character or set of characters. Once you have done a "begins with" match, it's not much of a leap to invert it to match items on the trailing side of a column's data. An example of this might be where you know that a certain set of rows has a name with the same word at the end. To perform an "ends with" match, the wild card is placed at the beginning of the criteria to tell the server to ignore all characters before it. The following example retrieves all accounts that have a name that ends with "Repair."

```
SELECT
    *
FROM
    tb_account
WHERE
    organization_name
LIKE '%Repair'
```

Contains

Among the most popular uses of the LIKE method is the matching of data that contains a certain character or set of characters. In this case the wildcard character is placed both before and after the criteria to tell the server to ignore any characters that come before or after the criteria. In the following example, all of the accounts with the word "boats" in their name are returned.

```
SELECT
    *
FROM
    tb_account
WHERE
    organization_name
LIKE '%boats%'
```

Intentional Mismatching (NOT)

You can eliminate certain rows from your result set by using the "not equal" operator or the NOT keyword. These options allow you to evaluate on negative logic. For example, you may wish to see all of the customer accounts that are not in a given state. Or you may wish to see all products that have a name that does not include a certain word. There are two ways to intentionally mismatch data in SQL. The first is to simply use a "not equal to" (<>) operator. This method works well with numeric values and complete text matches but is not suited for partial text matches. In the following example, all accounts are returned that are not in postal code 53708.

```
SELECT
    *
FROM
    tb_account
WHERE
    postal_code <> 53708
```

When you need to mismatch on criteria involving part of a string of characters, you need to use the LIKE keyword. Since the syntax for this keyword does not involve standard operators, you will need to use the NOT keyword with it. The NOT keyword can be used with a variety of other syntax to perform complex matching. It is not limited to use with the LIKE keyword. In the example below the statement will return all accounts that do not have the word "auto" in their names.

```
SELECT
    *
FROM
    tb_account
WHERE
    Organization_name NOT LIKE '%auto%'
```

Compound WHERE Clause Logic

In many cases it becomes necessary to combine matching logic. Sometimes the results that you desire will require you to mix two or more elements of logic in the WHERE clause. Keep in mind that typically the simpler the result, the more complex the SQL logic. For example, you might want to only include accounts that are not in one of two postal codes. To do this you will use the AND keyword to tell the WHERE clause of your statement that there is more than one piece of logic to evaluate. Such a statement would look like the following:

```
SELECT
    *
FROM
    tb_account
WHERE
    postal_code <> 53708
AND
    postal_code <> 07102
```

Using a Logical OR

It isn't unusual to find yourself in need of a WHERE clause that uses OR rather than AND as an operator. A logical OR operator can be used in the same way as a logical AND. It simply adds more logic to the WHERE clause that will be used in row selection by the server. You can also combine OR's and AND's together to get very specific results. The following statement is similar to the one that was shown before. However, this time all accounts that are in either of the two postal codes will be included. This is done by simply changing the AND to an OR and changing the operators.

```
SELECT
   *
FROM
   tb_account
WHERE
   postal_code = 53708
OR
   Postal_code = 07102
```

Sub-Queries – Nesting SELECT Statements

Sooner or later you will find yourself in a situation where you simply can not obtain the results that you want with the SQL syntax that you are trying to use. It is possible to create a SQL statement that seems like it should work but simply doesn't return the correct rows, or, in some cases, any rows at all. To address these types of needs, SQL includes capabilities for what are known as sub-queries in the statement syntax. There are a few different types of sub-queries, each of which addresses a specific type of problem.

At their heart sub-queries are designed to allow you to utilize two or more tables to obtain very specific results. It is not unusual to find that sub-queries accomplish the same objectives as joins. However, sub-queries can provide several solutions to problems that joins can not address. Common uses of sub-queries include the following:

- Looking Up Correlated Data—The matching of data from one table to data in a second table based on values from the first table.
- Looking Up Non-Correlated Data—The matching of data from one table to data in a second table based on specified criteria that are not present in the first table.
- Checking for existence—The ability to use data in one table as a test against data in another table to determine existence of certain rows.

Sub-queries involve the embedding of one SELECT statement inside of another. This is called "nesting" and is a common characteristic of most programming and scripting languages. By embedding a SELECT statement inside of your SQL syntax, you can perform a more complex match than otherwise might be achieved. Figure 5-1 illustrates how a sub-query works with a main query to perform a look up.

Figure 5-1 an illustration of how sub-queries work

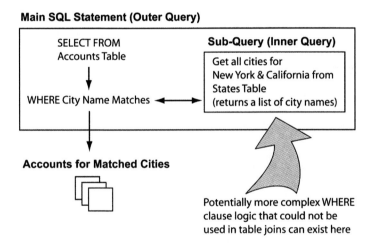

Main SQL Statement (Outer Query)

SELECT FROM
Accounts Table

Sub-Query (Inner Query)

Get all cities for
New York & California from
States Table
(returns a list of city names)

WHERE City Name Matches

Accounts for Matched Cities

Potentially more complex WHERE
clause logic that could not be
used in table joins can exist here

It's important to note that, in most cases, sub-queries do not solve problems that could not otherwise be resolved by using JOIN syntax in the SQL statement. The use of JOIN syntax in more efficient and should be considered first. However, there are situations where sub-queries solve problems that JOIN syntax can not address. In most cases these situations involve existence testing, but may include other scenarios.

Looking Up Correlated Data

Correlated sub-queries provide interaction between the main query and sub-query based on data that is passed from the main query. This type of sub-query uses data from the main query in its WHERE clause. This means that the sub-query will be executed for each row of the main query. While this adds overhead to the server, it also offers a solution to certain types of problems. For example, if you wanted to retrieve information in the sub-query based on a combination of data from the main query and other criteria, this type of query would work well. The following example shows how a sub-query allows for the selection of orders for companies in California whose company names include the word "services."

```
SELECT
    *
FROM
    tb_order
WHERE
    'CA' IN
    (
        SELECT
            region
        FROM
            tb_account
        WHERE
            tb_order.account_id = tb_account.account_id
        AND
            Organization_name LIKE '%services%'
    )
```

Notice that the sub-query is inside of parenthesis to keep it from being confused with the syntax of the main statement. Also, notice that the column names inside of the sub-query use fully-qualified names.

Looking Up Non-Correlated Data

Non-correlated sub-queries are simpler than their correlated counter parts in that they do not use data from the main query in their WHERE clause criteria.

```
SELECT
    *
FROM
    tb_order
WHERE
    account_id IN
(
    SELECT
        account_id
    FROM
        tb_account
    WHERE
        region = 'CA'
)
```

Evaluating for Existence

Another evaluation common to sub-queries involves the ability to determine if certain combinations of the logic represent any results at all. To evaluate for the existence of certain rows, you must use the EXISTS keyword in combination with a sub-query. Using the EXISTS key word allows you to return records in the main query based on matches or mismatches in the sub-query's results. In the following example, account information is returned for accounts that are located where prospects exist.

```
SELECT
   *
FROM
   tb_account
WHERE EXISTS
(
   SELECT
      *
   FROM
      tb_prospect
   WHERE
      tb_account.region = tb_prospect.state
)
```

By changing the logic (adding a NOT keyword) the same statement can be used to show account information where no prospects exist in the same regions.

```
SELECT
   *
FROM
   tb_account
WHERE NOT EXISTS
(
   SELECT
      *
   FROM
      tb_prospect
   WHERE
      tb_account.region = tb_prospect.state
)
```

Chapter 6:
Joining Tables

Without a doubt, you won't be using SQL very long before needing to join two or more tables together. This chapter provides detailed examples of how to perform a variety of table joins. Joining tables allows you to retrieve data from more than on table at a time. Joining tables is an optimized way of sub-querying data and is the preferred method for accessing related data from multiple tables. It is very important not to confuse SQL's table joining features with relational database table relationships. While the two are similar, joining tables offers data combinations from multiple tables. Table relationships exist for the purpose of imposing rules to maintain the integrity of related data across tables. Table relationships serve the purpose of enforcing Referential Integrity. With that understood, knowing how tables are related for the purpose of RI may also help you understand the proper fields to use when joining tables for the purpose of accessing combined table data.

There are a variety of ways that two or more tables can be joined together. Keeping in mind that the purpose of these methods is to access data from all of the tables, it's important to note that the wrong type of join will inevitably result in the wrong rows returned. There are six major types of table joins in SQL:

- Inner Join
- Left Outer Join
- Right Outer Join
- Full Outer Join
- Cross Join
- Union Join

Each of these join types will result in different row sets being returned from the database server. We will take a look at each of them. Where appropriate the ANSI92 (SQL2) and ANSI99 (SQL3) syntax has been provided. However, the examples are in the SQL3 syntax only.

Join Types vs. Join Operators

With the advent of SQL3 syntax, the idea of a join type is separated from the idea of an operator which represents how matching will be performed. In earlier versions of SQL, the way two tables were joined involved setting a column from the first table equal to (or compared in some other way) to a column from the second table in the WHERE clause. While this was straight forward, it lacked the more robust capabilities of being able to control the join type and the join operator at the same time. For example, an Inner Join in SQL2 required that records from both tables on the joined columns be equal in order for inclusion. With SQL3 the definition of an inner join is broader. It merely states that a match must exist on both sides for inclusion. The matching criteria are controlled by the operator which might be any of the standard scalar operators used in expressions (=, <=, <=, <>).

Inner (Equal) Joins

Inner Joins are likely the most common type of join. They are easy to understand and relatively easy to use. An Inner Join requires that a match exist on both sides of the join in order for any data from either table to be returned from the database server. Inner Joins are sometimes referred to as "Equal Joins" because the data on both sides must match. This is a somewhat out dated term since SQL3 syntax allows for inner joins using other operators besides the "equals" operator. The danger in using an Inner Join is that, if there isn't a match on either side, no rows are returned from either side. For example, if you are Inner Joining an Accounts table to an Orders table, an Account having no orders won't appear. This may not be what you want.

SQL3 Inner Join Syntax

```
SELECT
    ColumnName, ColumnName...
FROM
    TableName INNER JOIN TableName
ON
    TableName.ColumnName (=,<=,>=,<>) TableName.ColumnName
```

The following example shows an Inner Join between the tb_accounts and tb_orders table using an "equals" operator. In this case, if there are accounts with no orders, the account will be omitted from the result set.

```
SELECT
    *
FROM
    tb_account INNER JOIN tb_order
ON
    tb_account.account_id = tb_order.account_id
```

Notice that this statement uses fully qualified column names in the "ON" clause. This is required so that the database server knows how to join the tables. Also, the asterisk (*) in the SELECT clause indicates that all rows from both table will be returned. You could list the columns that you want from each table, but you would need to fully qualify any names that are the same in both tables.

SQL2 Inner Join Syntax

```
SELECT
   ColumnName, ColumnName...
FROM
   TableName, TableName
WHERE
   TableName.ColumnName = TableName.ColumnName
```

Left Outer Joins

Left Outer Joins solve some problems that Inner Joins pose. They don't restrict record selection on the left or the outer table. This is sometimes desirable, such as if you want to show a complete list of items in one column and only populate another column with matching rows from a different table. Left Outer Join syntax is similar to Inner Join Syntax. As with Inner Joins, the matching is controlled by the operator, not the join type, if you are using SQL3 syntax.

SQL3 Left Outer Join Syntax

```
SELECT
   ColumnName, ColumnName...
FROM
   TableName LEFT OUTER JOIN TableName
ON
   TableName.ColumnName (=,<=,>=,<>) TableName.ColumnName
```

A Left Outer join will include all of the rows from the left table and only the matching rows from the right table. In the following example, all accounts but only orders where there is a match to an account will be returned.

```
SELECT
    *
FROM
    tb_account LEFT OUTER JOIN tb_order
ON
    tb_account.account_id = tb_order.account_id
```

SQL2 Left Outer Join Syntax

```
SELECT
    ColumnName, ColumnName...
FROM
    TableName LEFT OUTER JOIN TableName
WHERE
    TableName.ColumnName *= TableName.ColumnName
```

Right Outer Joins

Right Outer Joins, as you might expect, are exactly the opposite of Left Outer Joins. The only difference is that all of the rows from the right table will be included while only the matching rows from the left table will be included. This join type is really a matter of convenience but can save you some typing.

SQL3 Right Outer Join Syntax

Syntax for using the RIGHT command

```
SELECT
    ColumnName, ColumnName...
FROM
    TableName RIGHT OUTER JOIN TableName
ON
    TableName.ColumnName (=,<=,>=,<>) TableName.ColumnName
```

In the following example, we simply reverse the logic so that all orders are returned even if they don't have a matching account. Only those accounts with orders will be included in the results. This is a good way to find "orphaned" order records.

```
SELECT
    *
FROM
    tb_account RIGHT OUTER JOIN tb_order
ON
    tb_account.account_id = tb_order.account_id
```

SQL2 Right Outer Join Syntax

```
SELECT
    ColumnName, ColumnName...
FROM
    TableName, TableName
ON
    TableName.ColumnName =* TableName.ColumnName
```

Full Outer Joins

A Full Outer join will include all of the unmatched rows from both the left and right tables. It is the combination of a Left Outer and Right Outer join. For example if you wanted a listing of all accounts and orders where either table failed to have a match in the other you would use a full outer join. You might want to do this to find orphaned records in both tables so that you could clean up the data.

SQL3 Full Outer Join Syntax

```
SELECT
    ColumnName, ColumnName...
FROM
    TableName FULL OUTER JOIN TableName
ON
    TableName.ColumnName = TableName.ColumnName
```

In the following example all records from both tables that fail to match the other table will be returned.

```
SELECT
    *
FROM
    tb_account FULL OUTER JOIN tb_order
ON
    tb_account.account_id = tb_order.account_id
```

SQL2 Full Outer Join Syntax

```
SELECT
    [DISTINCT] [*] ColumnName, ColumnName...
FROM
    TableName1, TableName2
ON
    TableName1.ColumnName *=* TableName2.ColumnName
WHERE
    ...
```

Cross Joins (Cartesian Products)

A Cross Join produces what is known as a Cartesian product. This is every possible combination of data from both sides of the join. For example, if you wanted to show all customers with all order information and all orders with all customer information in a result set this is the type of join you would chose. The way this is done is to multiply the number of rows from the second table by the number of rows in the first table. Obviously, cross joins can produce an excessive amount of data, so they should only be used in situations where they are absolutely necessary.

SQL3 Cross Join Syntax

```
SELECT
    ColumnName, ColumnName...
FROM
    TableName CROSS JOIN TableName
```

In the following example, all rows from the tb_accounts and tb_orders tables will be returned in one set of results.

```
SELECT
    *
FROM
    tb_account CROSS JOIN tb_order
```

SQL2 Cross Join Syntax

```
SELECT
    ColumnName, ColumnName...
FROM
    TableName, TableName
```

Joining on More Than One Column

In some cases you may need to join two tables on more than one column to get the desired results. This can happen when the database is not well engineered or when you simply need to get an unusual combination of data.

SQL3 Multi-Column Join Syntax

```
SELECT
    ColumnName, ColumnName...
FROM
    TableName INNER JOIN TableName
ON
    Table1.ColumnName = Table2.ColumnName
AND
    Table1.ColumnName = Table2.ColumnName
```

In the following example, the SQL statement will return only those rows from both tables where an account and a prospect exist in the same city and state. In this case a distinct list of cities and states are returned, but any columns from either table could have been included.

```
SELECT
    DISTINCT tb_account.city, tb_account.region
FROM
    tb_account inner Join tb_prospect
ON
    tb_account.region = tb_prospect.state
AND
    tb_account.city = tb_prospect.city
```

SQL2 Multi Column Join Syntax

```
SELECT
   ColumnName, ColumnName...
FROM
   TableName,TableName
WHERE
   Table1.ColumnName = Table2.ColumnName
AND
   Table1.ColumnName = Table2.ColumnName
```

Joining Multiple Tables

It isn't unusual to have a need to join 3 or more tables together. Multitable joins are part of the benefit and a requirement for SQL databases. It's important to remember that, once two tables are joined, a row set has been established. The addition of a third table will, in effect, be a matter of joining the third table to the row set that was created by the first two tables. This means that the order in which the joins occur matters.

SQL3 Multi-Table Join Syntax

```
SELECT
   ColumnName, ColumnName...
FROM
   Table1Name1 INNER JOIN TableName2
ON
   Table1.ColumnName = Table2.ColumnName
INNER JOIN
   TableName3
ON
   Table2.ColumnName = Table3.ColumnName
AND
   Table1.ColumnName = Table2.ColumnName
```

In the following example, the tb_account, tb_prospect, and tb_order tables are all joined to produce a row set that shows all orders that were placed in cities where there were accounts or prospects. Since Left Outer Joins were used, any city-state combination that includes a prospect or account will show up without regards for the placement of orders.

```
SELECT
    tb_account.city, tb_account.region,
    tb_account.organization_name,
    tb_order.order_id, tb_order.date_placed
FROM
    tb_account LEFT OUTER JOIN tb_prospect
ON
    tb_account.region = tb_prospect.state
AND
    tb_account.city = tb_prospect.city
LEFT OUTER JOIN
    tb_order
ON
    tb_account.account_id = tb_order.account_id
```

SQL2 Multi-Table Join Syntax

```
SELECT
    ColumnName, ColumnName...
FROM
    TableName,TableName
WHERE
    Table1.ColumnName = Table2.ColumnName
AND
    Table1.ColumnName = Table2.ColumnName
AND
    Table1.ColumnName = Table2.ColumnName
```

Joining Vertically (UNION joins)

In some cases you may need to obtain results from two tables where the columns match each other and where you want a single set of columns with the data from both tables included as a single row set. With most SQL joins, the selected columns from both tables are combined to produce results that include a combination of columns from both tables. You might think of this as a horizontal join because it is like setting the data from both tables next to each other and matching it up. Inner and outer joins work this way. In these cases you will usually see data duplicated from one or more of the tables. For example, if you combine the columns of the Accounts table with the columns of the Orders table, each account will be duplicated if there is more than one Order for any given account. The following example shows how that data might look:

```
Account Name        Order Number
-----------         -----------
Account1            Order1
Account1            Order2
Account1            Order3
Account2            Order4
Account2            Order5
```

However, if you had two tables with similar types of data and you wanted to combine them so that a single list of rows was created for a single list of columns, a conventional join would not work. To accomplish this, a UNION Join is used. The following example shows how data from a UNION Join might look:

```
Account Name        Order Number
-----------         -----------
Table1Account       Table1Order
Table1Account       Table1Order
Table1Account       Table1Order
Table2Account       Table2Order
Table2Account       Table2Order
```

SQL3 Union Join Syntax

```
SELECT
    ColumnName, ColumnName...
FROM
    TableName,TableName
WHERE
    ...

UNION

SELECT
    ColumnName, ColumnName...
FROM
    TableName,TableName
WHERE
    ...
```

A UNION Join allows you to stack the results from two or more SELECT statements on top of each other. For this to work the column names *are similar* must be the same and data types returned from each SELECT statement must be the same. In the following example accounts and prospects are combined into one set of results. The names of some columns have been aliased so that they match the corresponding column names from the other SELECT statement.

```
SELECT
    organization_name, city, region, 'Account' as type
FROM
    tb_account

UNION

SELECT
    company_name as organization_name,
    city, state as region, 'Prospect' as type
FROM
    tb_prospect
```

Notice that a string constant has been added and named "Type." This allows you to identify the table each row came from. UNION Joins are powerful tools and will even allow you to convert data types in one SELECT statement to match that of another. They do not require that the tables be of identical structure, only that the results from each SELECT statement are. UNION Joins can even be used with SELECT statements that include other types of joins as long at the results for both SELECT statements are the same.

SQL2 UNION Join Syntax

There are no difference between SQL2 and SQL3 for a UNION Join. However, the SELECT portions of the statement must comply with the relevant SQL2 requirements for join and other aspects of the statements.

Chapter 7:
Summarizing & Deriving Data

SQL provides a means by which you can derive values from the data stored in various tables. It isn't uncommon to find that at least some of the desired information isn't stored in the database but is available by utilizing various values that are stored in the database. An example might be an amount multiplied by a sales tax factor. Another example might be the concatenation of a first, middle, and last name so that a person's full name is returned. Deriving data is a simple matter of writing an expression that will assemble, calculate, and return the desired results. An expression is simply a combination of SQL syntax that allows you to combine column values with constant values to create a new value. The example below shows a simple expression that adds a constant numerical value of 5% to an amount:

```
tb_product.unit_price * 1.05
```

There are several different types of derived values that you can create using SQL. They include that ability to perform math operations as shown above. They also include the ability to manipulate string values to assemble different types of words, phrases, or names. Expressions can also be used to convert data types. For example, you may wish to show a numeric value as part of a string value. SQL provides a CONVERT capability for this purpose. Other derived values may also include the use of SQL aggregate functions that perform summarization of data like sub-totaling, averaging, and other summary functions.

This chapter will cover several different ways to derive values from your SQL database. We will take a closer look at the following topics:

- Manipulating String Values
- Performing Math Operations
- Manipulating Dates and Times
- Summarizing Data with Aggregate Functions

Manipulating String Values

In order to search various character data (string values), many databases are structured to store individual elements of a phase or name in separate columns. Sometimes, string values and numeric values are combined in character-based columns, and the numeric value is needed without the string values. For these types of reasons, SQL includes the ability to manipulate character values (strings) in a variety of ways. Some of the most common include the following:

- Concatenation—The combining of two or more strings to produce a multi-word phrase or name
- Parsing—The ability to retrieve part of a string value
- Trimming—The ability to remove leading or trailing blank spaces

In the example below all three of these features are used to produce a derived value from several character fields:

```
SELECT
   organization_name,

RTRIM(tb_account_contact.first_name) + ' ' + LTRIM(tb_
account_contact.last_name) AS Contact,

LEFT(phone, 3) + '-' + RIGHT(LEFT(phone, 6), 3) + '-' +
RIGHT(phone, 4) AS Phone

FROM
   tb_account INNER JOIN tb_account_contact
ON
   tb_account.account_id = tb_account_contact.account_id
```

The following is a sampling of the data that this statement will return:

```
organization_name              Contact           Phone
------------------------------------------------------------
Metro Appliance Service    Bela Bellatauno   608-601-5139
MedicServe Medical Supply  Bartlett Belmonti 585-294-6230
MedicServe Medical Supply  Avery Beerman     524-135-1498
MedicServe Medical Supply  Barry Belster     415-840-9283
MedicServe Medical Supply  Barrett Bequin    659-246-4534
Marcy Elaine Bakery        Austin Bedini     569-122-9530
Marcy Elaine Bakery        Arvel Bederman    844-281-1369
```

To better understand this statement, let's take a look at each part of the SELECT clause. The first column is a standard column name that returns the organization name. However, the other columns are expressions that utilize several string manipulations.

RTIM, LTRIM, and Concatenation

```
RTRIM(tb_account_contact.first_name) + ' ' + LTRIM(tb_
account_contact.last_name) AS Contact,
```

In this portion of the statement, we are retrieving the value of the first_name field. To make sure there are no trailing blank spaces, it has been placed inside of an RTRIM function. This will strip any trailing blank spaces. This is important because we want the last_name field to appear exactly one space after the first name field, and some column data types (like char) will append trailing spaces to the data by default. The plus signs and single quotes (+ ' ' +) append a single blank space as a string constant to the expression. The plus signs will append strings or perform addition on numeric values. The LTRIM simply removes any leading spaces from the last_name field and finally the entire expression is aliased as the name "Contact".

LEFT, RIGHT, and String Parsing

```
LEFT(phone, 3) + '-' + RIGHT(LEFT(phone, 6), 3) + '-' +
RIGHT(phone, 4) AS Phone
```

In the next portion of the statement, the LEFT function is used to extract the left 3 characters from the phone column. The phone number is stored in the database without any dashes or parenthesis. This expression will add a dash (-) between each part of the phone number to make it easier to read. It's important to know that when there are multiple sets of parenthesis the inner most set is processed first. The first RIGHT function is operating on the LEFT function results that are inside of the RIGHT function parenthesis. That means that the first 6 characters are retrieved and then the last three of the first six are returned. This retrieves the prefix of the phone number without the area code. Finally, the last 4 characters are retrieved and appended with a dash in the right spot. The end result is an expression column named "Phone" with a fully formatted phone number as its value.

Performing Math Operations

SQL also provides a robust and relatively complete expression language for performing mathematical operations on the data. This includes the ability to add, subtract, multiply, and divide. The standard mathematical operators are used to do this as they would in most computer languages or scripts. The following example shows several mathematical operations that result in derived data.

```
SELECT
    product_name, unit_cost, unit_price,
    ((unit_price - unit_cost) / unit_price) * 100 AS
profit_percent
FROM
    tb_product
```

This statement will return results that look like the following:

```
product_name                      unit_cost unit_price profit_percent
------------------------------------------------------------------
Copier Model 100, 20 sheet,   75        97.5        23.07
Copier Model 220, 40 sheet,   125       162.5       23.07
Copier Model 555, 40 sheet,   375       487.5       23.07
8.5X11 Reem Std. Office Paper 0.75      0.975       23.07
8.5X11 Reem Recycled Office   0.7       0.91        23.07
10X14 Poster Board (foam)     1.25      1.625       23.07
```

Notice that the unit_price – unit_cost expression is inside of an inner set of parenthesis. This means it will be done first. Once that value is obtained, it will be divided by (/) the unit_price. This will yield a fractional value that, when multiplied (*) by 100, will show as the profit percentage for the line item with a name of "profit_percent." These types of math operations are very common, and the database server is a good place to have them performed.

Manipulating Dates & Times

Databases store date and time values in a unique way to allow for their use in expressions. Most modern databases store dates and times together in a single column that has a "date/time" data type. This means that date, time, or both date and time values can be stored in such a column. If a date is stored with no specific time, most databases will default the time portion of the column to midnight at zero seconds, which represents the first instant of a given day. It's important to remember that, even though your database may include the ability to store date/time values, the person who designed your database may have chosen a different method. For example some developers store dates in integer fields or character fields. If this is done, you will have to use expressions to convert and parse the values.

When dates and times are stored in date/time columns, you will have the ability to operate on them in expressions. This means you can perform what is sometimes referred to as "date math." This is the ability to calculate differentials from a given date and/or time.

The following example shows how you can add a numeric value to a date/time column. It shows orders with the date each order is placed and then the same date plus one day. Note that the numeric constant could be a fraction of a day in which case the time value portion of the field would change rather than the date value.

```
SELECT
   order_id,
   date_placed,
   date_placed + 1 AS follow_up_date
FROM
   tb_order
```

Here are the sample results from the above statement:

order_id	date_placed	follow_up_date
206	12/29/2001 1:53:07 PM	12/30/2001 1:53:07 PM
207	11/5/2003 6:01:24 PM	11/6/2003 6:01:24 PM
215	8/4/2003 1:01:24 AM	8/5/2003 1:01:24 AM
230	1/7/2001 4:34:39 PM	1/8/2001 4:34:39 PM

You can also use two different date values in an expression to determine the difference between them. In this case you might not be using a constant value like in the last example. The two date values might be data from separate columns. While not part of the ANSI standard, most manufacturers like Microsoft and Oracle have added date/time functions to extend the SQL language capabilities for manipulating dates and times. Such functions typically include the ability to determine the difference between two dates and/or times.

Summarizing Data with Aggregate Functions

Since SQL isn't a full-blown programming language, it lacks some of the control structures and looping capabilities that programmers commonly use to summarize data. However, SQL does include many summary functions that perform these types of operations on the database server for you. These functions are relatively easy to use and perform well. They make SQL a great tool for getting answers to certain types of questions concerning things like sums, subtotals, counts, and the like. Aggregate functions allow you to perform summary operations on column data from one or more tables. They can be combined with join syntax and other aspects of SQL to produced highly customized results. Aggregating data can include a variety of functions including the following:

- Summing Data (totaling)
- Counting Rows (records)
- Averaging Data
- Getting a Maximum or Minimum Value

SUM (Totaling Data)

Summing numerical values is among the most common use of an aggregate function in SQL. It allows you to add up all of the values in a given column and for certain rows. The SQL syntax for performing a sum is simple. You simply type in the word "SUM" with parenthesis following it. Then you put the column name inside of the parenthesis. The following example illustrates the use of the SUM function. In this case we have joined four tables to get the unit price amount and summed it for all orders in the system. This would be thought of as a grand total since the number represents a single value for all orders. You can add the DISTINCT keyword to make sure that duplicates are omitted from the results. However, it may not always make sense to do this. The DISTINCT keyword would be placed inside of the parenthesis before the column name that is to be summed. For example:

```
SUM(DISTINCT unit_price)

SELECT
    SUM(unit_price) AS total_price_all_orders
FROM
    tb_account INNER JOIN tb_order
ON
    tb_account.account_id = tb_order.account_id
INNER JOIN
    tb_order_item
ON
    tb_order_item.order_id = tb_order.order_id
INNER JOIN
    tb_product
ON
    tb_product.product_id = tb_order_item.product_id
```

The results will only return one row and one column with the numeric value representing the total because the aggregate value is the only item in the SELECT portion of the statement.

```
total_price_all_orders
----------------------
             87759.178
```

COUNT (Counting Rows)

SQL also provides a function for counting rows. This can be helpful for a variety of situations. Like the SUM function, the COUNT function simply requires that a column name be provided within the parenthesis. A single column and row will be returned with the number of rows matching the criteria in the rest of the SQL statement. You can optionally add the DISTINCT keyword to make sure that duplicates are omitted from the results. In the following example, the SUM function from the last example has be changed to use the COUNT function.

```
SELECT
    COUNT(DISTINCT unit_price) AS total_number_of_order_
items
FROM
    tb_account INNER JOIN tb_order
ON
    tb_account.account_id = tb_order.account_id
INNER JOIN
    tb_order_item
ON
    tb_order_item.order_id = tb_order.order_id
INNER JOIN
    tb_product
ON
    tb_product.product_id = tb_order_item.product_id
```

The results will show the following:

```
total_number_of_order_items
---------------------------
                         23
```

AVG (Averaging Amounts)

Averaging is another aggregate function that is built into SQL and offers an easy way to get important summarized information from the database server. The AVG command will automatically calculate the average of a value by performing a SUM and COUNT behind the scenes. Again, to use the AVG function you simply place the column that you wish to average inside of the parenthesis. You can optionally add the DINTINCT keyword to make sure that duplicates are omitted from the results. The following example shows the average unit price of all orders.

```
SELECT
    AVG(DISTINCT unit_price) AS average_unit_price
FROM
    tb_account INNER JOIN tb_order
ON
    tb_account.account_id = tb_order.account_id
INNER JOIN
    tb_order_item
ON
    tb_order_item.order_id = tb_order.order_id
INNER JOIN
    tb_product
ON
    tb_product.product_id = tb_order_item.product_id
```

The results will show the following:

```
average_unit_price
------------------
            95.64
```

MAX (Getting the Maximum Value of a Column)

In some cases it may be desirable to find out the maximum or minimum value of a column given the criteria of the SQL statement. For example, you may wish to know the highest order amount or the highest line item amount. Or you may wish to know the last sequence number to be used. Conversely you may wish to find the lowest or minimum amount of something. To help with these kinds of questions, SQL includes two functions (MAX and MIN) that will retrieve the highest or lowest value from a column. These commands will operate on numeric, string, and date/time columns. The following example returns two values. They include the maximum unit price of all items in all orders and the minimum unit price of all items in all orders.

```
SELECT
   MAX(unit_price) AS max_unit_price,
   MIN(unit_price) AS min_unit_price
FROM
   tb_account INNER JOIN tb_order
ON
   tb_account.account_id = tb_order.account_id
INNER JOIN
   tb_order_item
ON
   tb_order_item.order_id = tb_order.order_id
INNER JOIN
   tb_product
ON
   tb_product.product_id = tb_order_item.product_id
```

The results will show the following:

```
max_unit_price          min_unit_price
-----------------------------------------
          5.5                    0.91
```

Grouping & Sub-Totaling (GROUP BY)

In many cases a simple grand total does not meet the need at hand. Using aggregate functions in the manner we've shown so far only returns summarized data for the entire row set. While you can add WHERE clause logic to control the number and type of rows returned, you can not perform sub-totaling in this way. In order to show multiple summarized values at various levels in your results, you must group the data. By establishing groups you have the ability to create sub-totals at each grouping level. Conventional SQL only produces grouping of data for the purpose of sub-totaling. To do this you will use the GROUP BY clause. This feature allows you to create groupings on the data based on all of the columns that are included in the SELECT clause. It is important to note that GROUP BY has two requirements:

- GROUP BY will group on all non-aggregate columns identified in the SELECT clause. The groupings will be unique to the combination of columns. You can not group by less columns than what you show in the SELECT clause.

- GROUP BY requires that you have at least one aggregate function expression defined in SELECT clause

The following example creates a list of orders and shows their associated order amounts. The order amount is not a value that is stored in the database. It must be derived by adding up all of the order items for each order. This is typical of a normalized data structure and a good example of where the GROUP BY clause can be beneficial.

```
SELECT
    tb_order.order_id,
    tb_order.date_placed AS order_date,
    SUM(unit_price) AS order_amount
FROM
    tb_account INNER JOIN tb_order
ON
    tb_account.account_id = tb_order.account_id
INNER JOIN
    tb_order_item
ON
    tb_order_item.order_id = tb_order.order_id
INNER JOIN
    tb_product
ON
    tb_product.product_id = tb_order_item.product_id
WHERE
    tb_account.region = 'CA'
GROUP BY
    tb_order.order_id,
    tb_order.date_placed
```

This SQL statement will return a listing of all orders with their ID, date, and amount as shown below:

```
order_id    order_date              order_amount
-------------------------------------------------
248         6/19/2003 9:06:21       601.653
265         1/8/2002 8:54:36        269.035
277         8/20/2003 12:01:1       1017.185
285         1/9/2002 8:59:41        451.62
288         5/21/2002 6:59:52       649.883
```

Controlling Group Selection (HAVING)

The aggregate functions in SQL represent values that are not stored in the database. For this reason a conventional WHERE clause can not be used to control the selection criteria for summarized columns. In its place, the HAVING clause has been added to allow you to control the results based on the derived value of an aggregated column. This means that if you want to get the order total for all orders but only wanted it to include orders of $300 or greater the HAVING clause would allow you to do this. The following example shows the syntax for such a situation.

```
SELECT
    SUM(unit_price) AS total_price_all_orders
FROM
    tb_account INNER JOIN tb_order
ON
    tb_account.account_id = tb_order.account_id
INNER JOIN
    tb_order_item
ON
    tb_order_item.order_id = tb_order.order_id
INNER JOIN
    tb_product
ON
    tb_product.product_id = tb_order_item.product_id
WHERE
    tb_account.region = 'CA'
HAVING
    SUM(unit_price) > 300
```

The HAVING clause does not need to be applied to all aggregate columns if there is more than one and may be used with GROUP BY as well. It is important to note that HAVING does not replace the WHERE clause. They serve separate purposes. The WHERE clause allows for filtering on columns that are defined in the database as objects. The HAVING clause allows for filtering on columns that are derived from aggregated functions like SUM, COUNT, and AVG.

Chapter 8:
Managing Data

SQL not only provides an efficient and powerful set of methods for retrieving data in its data management language (DML) but also provides extensive data management capabilities. This includes the ability to INSERT, UPDATE, and DELETE data. The management of data is an important topic because data is frequently added to database tables in a manner that is inconsistent or incorrect. This is especially true with the recent advent of Web based applications that are used to collect information from users and frequently don't provide a sufficient means of validating data. Examples of this might include phone numbers that are entered in different ways, improperly spelled names and titles, and invalid dates. This chapter will focus on the use of the three main SQL statement types that allow for the creating, maintenance, and removal of data from SQL tables.

It's important to note that these capabilities are usually associated with certain security rights. You may not have the appropriate rights on your production database to perform these operations. If this is the case, you will typically get a message from the database server indicating that you have insufficient rights. You may need to contact your database administrator in such a case. The reason for the security on these operations is obvious. We would not want everyone with access to a given database to be able to remove or alter data.

The three main SQL statement types that allow for the management of data in SQL database tables include the following:

- INSERT—allows you to add new rows to an existing table.

- UPDATE—allows you to change the column values in an existing table's rows.

- DELETE—allows you to remove complete rows from an existing table.

Inserting New Data

INSERT Statement Syntax

```
INSERT [INTO] TableName
    (ColumnName, ColumnName...)
VALUES
    (Value1, Value2...)
```

The INSERT statement is used to create new records (rows) in a SQL database table. The syntax for inserting new rows into a table is fairly straight forward and involves defining the table to which you want to add data, the column names that you wish to populate, and your new row values that are to be placed in each of the columns. This is accomplished by defining the specific columns by name and their associated values. It is not necessary to add values to all columns if the table is structured in a way to allow NULL values in some of the columns (the ones that do not wish to populate). However, some columns will likely require a value and, in some cases, the value that you place in a column may have to be unique. This means that it can not be the same value that is found in the same column for any other row in the table. The following SQL statement adds a new customer to the Customers table.

```
INSERT INTO
    tb_account
    (account_id, organization_name, street_1,
    city, region, country)
VALUES
    (999999, 'Test Organization Name', '123 Street',
'Any City', 'CA', 'US')
```

> *Tip: If you do not set a value for a column that does not allow NULL, then the statement will fail. It's a good idea to check the database schema before issuing INSERT or UPDATE statements. The database schema is the definition of the database structure including its tables and columns.*

It is important to note that the values in this example above are shown with the appropriate special characters so that they are passed as the correct data types. The Value for the account_id column is passed as a numeric value without quotes around it. The other values have single quotes around them so that they are passed as string values. Also notice that the order the columns are shown in is the same order that the values are listed. This order must match in both parts of the statement to assure the correct values are placed in the corresponding columns.

Updating Existing Data

UPDATE Statement Syntax

```
UPDATE TableName SET
   ColumnName = Value,
   ColumnName = Value,
WHERE
   . . .
```

Updating data is very simple with SQL. You issue an UPDATE statement where you define the name of the table that you wish to update and then SET the various columns to corresponding values. The values that you pass must be the right data type for the column into which you are placing them. You don't have to update all of the columns in a given row or set of rows, and you can use a WHERE clause to control which rows get updated. If you do not set a value for a column that does not allow NULL, the statement will fail. It's a good idea to check the database schema before issuing INSERT or UPDATE statements.

In the following example, the row that represents account ID 999999 is found and updated. The account_id column is updated along with various other columns. Again notice that the correct special characters are used to pass the correct data types to each column. This is also a good example of how you can use the WHERE clause to control which rows get updated. Be very careful issuing UPDATE statements. If the WHERE clause information is not provided then all rows in the table will be updated.

```
UPDATE
   tb_account
SET
   account_id = 888888,
   organization_name = 'My New Organization Name',
   street_1 = '345 Street'
WHERE
   account_id = 999999
```

It's a good idea to use the WHERE clause criteria in a SELECT statement before you attempt to update the rows. This will show you the rows that will be affected by the UPDATE statement so that you can verify the WHERE clause criteria fist.

Deleting Data

DELETE Statement Syntax

```
DELETE FROM
   TableName
WHERE
   . . .
```

The DELETE statement allows you to remove one or more rows based on filtering that you define using a WHERE clause. The DELETE statement is relatively simple and easy to use. However, it is also potentially devastating to your data. Be especially careful when using it. As with the UPDATE statement, it's a good idea to use the WHERE clause criteria in a SELECT statement before you attempt to delete rows. This will show you the rows that will be removed by the DELETE statement so that you can verify the WHERE clause criteria fist.

The following example deletes all rows from the Customer table that have the phrase "Result Data" somewhere in the CompanyName column.

```
DELETE FROM
   tb_account
WHERE
   Organization_name LIKE '%Result Data%'
```

If you left off the WHERE clause as shown below all rows would be deleted from the table.

```
DELETE FROM
   tb_account
```

Chapter 9:
Basic Data Definitions (DDL)

Most modern database management systems include graphical user interfaces that allow you to define and manage the database structure. This includes the creation of tables and columns and the defining of column data types and other characteristics. However, data definition is part of the SQL standard and can be performed by using SQL statements. This chapter will provide a brief overview of the part of the SQL language that facilitates database definitions. This is known as Data Definition Language (DDL).

Creating Tables

Among the most common data definition tasks is the creation of tables. Tables store all of the user data in a database system. It is not unusual to encounter the need to create new tables as an organization's need to collect and use new types of information increases. To create tables you use the CREATE statement. The CREATE command is used to create a variety of database objects, not just tables. The following example shows the basic syntax for using the CREATE command to create a table.

Syntax for Creating a Table

```
CREATE TABLE TableName
  (
  Col1 DataType [NULL|NOT NULL] [DEFAULT default_value],
  Col2 DataType [NULL|NOT NULL] [DEFAULT default_value],
  Col3 DataType [NULL|NOT NULL] [DEFAULT default_value]
  )
```

When creating a table you must specify all columns and the attributes for each column. This includes the data type, NULL constraint, and default value for the column. The data type must be one of the supported data types for the type of database with which you are working. The most common SQL data types include:

- **CHAR: TEXT or STRING** (alphanumeric characters in fixed length)
- **VARCHAR:** (like Char, but variable length)
- **INT: INTEGER** (whole numbers only)
- **CURRENCY or MONEY** (floating point numbers with 4 decimal places)
- **DOUBLE: or FLOAT** (floating point number with X decimal places)
- **DATETIME:** (combination of date & time – will hold just date)
- **BIT: BOOLEAN or BIT** (a true/false value)

In the following example, we create a table with four columns. The first column is defined as an integer data type that does not allow NULL values and will set a default value of zero if no value is defined when rows are inserted. The other columns are defined as character or variable length character data types which require a length.

```
CREATE TABLE my_new_table
  (
  company_id int NOT NULL DEFAULT 0,
  company_name varchar(30),
  street1 varchar(30),
  city char(20)
  )
```

Changing the Structure of a Table

While it isn't desirable, it may, from time to time, be necessary to change the way a table is structured. That is to say it may be necessary to add, remove, or change columns in the table. SQL provides a means for doing this with the ALTER TABLE command. This command will allow you to add, change or drop columns from an existing table structure. Most databases will allow you to add a column without impacting the data in the existing columns. However, if you alter or drop a column in a table, data may be, and most likely will be, lost. For this reason you may wish to copy the table data before attempting to change a table's structure. You may also want to assure that the table is not being used by others.

Adding a Column

To add a column use the ALTER TABLE command in conjunction with an ADD command and the column attributes. The following example shows how to add a VARCHAR column to an existing table.

```
ALTER TABLE my_new_table
ADD phone VARCHAR(20) NOT NULL DEFAULT 'no phone number'
```

It's unlikely that you will be able to add a column to a table with existing data if the column does not allow NULL values. This is because the existing rows in the table will not have values for the new column.

They will default to NULL unless you specify a default value when adding the column.

Removing a Column

It is relatively easy to remove a column from a table. Keep in mind that this will result in the loss of all data in the column for all rows in the table. The following example shows how to DROP a column from an existing table.

```
ALTER TABLE my_new_table
DROP COLUMN phone
```

Changing a Column

To change the structure of a column you must drop it and add it again with different attributes. Some manufacturers have extended the ANSI standard for SQL to make this easier, but, by default, SQL3 does not include the ability to alter the structure of a column. Even if it did it is unlikely that the data would be maintained.

Dropping Tables

Like removing columns, removing tables is very easy to do. However, in this case, once the table is removed so is all of its associated data. Be careful when removing database tables. It's always a good idea to confirm that you have a backup of the data before performing such a task. The following example shows the removal of a table.

```
DROP TABLE my_new_table
```

Creating Indexes

Indexes are very important and frequently overlooked aspects of a table structure. An index is a duplication of certain data. By duplicating certain columns and referencing the duplicates back to the main table, the data in the main table can sorted and searched by the database server very rapidly. Indexes can also be used to force uniqueness on columns. Since SQL databases are "set" based, they tend to have problems when two rows in a table are identical. For this reason, it is always a good idea to have what is known as a Primary Key on every table. A Primary Key will ensure that all rows have some unique combination of column data. It also serves to create relationships between tables to enforce referential integrity.

To create an index you will issue a CREATE command. However, in this case, you will add the "INDEX" keyword and the name of the new index. There is also an option to make the index unique. Finally, you must indicate the table and column name on which the index is to be created, and you should also show if the sort order of the index should be ascending (ASC) or descending (DESC). In some cases a descending index is desirable. For example, when you want to show the most recent date first on a date/time column.

Syntax for Creating Indexes

```
CREATE [UNIQUE] INDEX IndexName
ON TableName.ColumnName [ASC, DESC]
```

Or for compound indexes

```
CREATE [UNIQUE] INDEX IndexName
ON TableName (ColumnName [ASC, DESC], ColumnName [ASC,
DESC])
```

In some cases you may wish to create a compound index or what is sometimes called a composite index. This is an index that operates on more than one column. For example you might want a list of people's names sorted by last name and then, within last name, sub-sorted by first name. In the following example a compound index is created which is sorted first on the country column and within country by region. Both columns are sorted in ascending order because no specific order is defined. Ascending order is the default.

```
CREATE INDEX idx_test
ON
tb_account (country, region)
```

If the UNIQUE keyword had been added after the CREATE command, the database would not allow more than one entry in the account table that had the same country and region. If such entries already existed, the attempt to create this index would fail.

Dropping Indexes

To drop an index from the database, you must indicate the name of the index and the table on which it was created. Simply naming the index will not work because it is possible to have more than on index with the same name on different tables. The following is the syntax structure and an example of how to drop an index from a table.

Syntax:

```
DROP INDEX TableName.IndexName
```

Example:

```
DROP INDEX tb_account.idx_test
```

Creating Table Relationships & Constraints

The ability to define relationships between tables is one of the benefits of using a relational database management system. While this feature is often overlooked, it can add significant value. Table relationships serve two primary purposes. First, they help database users, programmers, report designers, and analysts understand how the database is structured. Second, and more importantly, they facilitate constraints. Constraints are attributes that you can associate with a table or table relationship that force certain rules to be applied to the way in which the data is inserted, updated, and deleted. This is commonly referred to as Referential Integrity because it addresses concerns about how data in one table relates to data in other tables.

Referential Integrity constraints can be added at the same time that table relationships are defined. This is sometimes done by using a database manufacturer's graphical user interface, but it can also be done using SQL-DDL commands. Before we dive into creating table relationships and Referential Integrity constraints, let's take a closer look at what they are and how they work.

Table Relationships

Tables can be related to each other in a formal way so that data in one table is maintained on the basis of data in another table. We sometimes think of this as a parent-child relationship, but this comparison is not completely accurate since a table can have any number of parent tables associated with it and can be a parent to any number of child tables. In order for table relationships to exist, there must be a primary key (PK) defined on the first table and foreign key (FK) defined on the second table. For this reason, we typically think of the first table as the primary table and the second table as the foreign table. Primary and foreign keys are special types of indexes that facilitate table relationships. They have special attributes that are not necessarily associated with normal indexes.

Primary Keys

Primary Keys are a means to establish a unique identifier for each row in the primary table. They must enforce uniqueness and may not allow NULL values. That is to say, when you define a primary key for a table, the columns that constitute that key will have to hold unique values for every row in the table, and they must hold some defined value (they can not be empty). These rules represent what we call a "primary key constraint" because they constrain how data may be added to the table.

Some experts in database design suggest that the values that are stored in primary key columns should be generated on "meaningless" basis. This is actually a very good idea. Since primary key values must, by definition, be unique there is a temptation to use what is sometimes viewed as a unique identifier as the value for such columns. For example, most people in the United States believe that a government issued social security number (SSN) is a unique number only assigned once. To many this makes it a candidate for a primary key on a database table. However, if you speak with information systems professionals who work for the state or federal government, you will learn that it is possible for two people to be issued the same SSN. It is also possible for a SSN to be changed. I have heard that this has, in fact, happened. That would create a big problem for your database if you use SSN as a primary key value. A meaningless key can always be unique and unchanged because it is meaningless and serves no other purpose. Another way to look at it is to consider that a meaningless value—like a system generated number—would not represent any inherent information about the row in the database to which it is assigned. It would by your unique record number for each entry in the table and, therefore, would not represent the potential for problems down the road.

To create a primary key, you may either define it at the time that table is created or after the table is created. The following example shows how to alter an existing table by adding a primary key on the account_id column. The primary key name is PK01 but could have been different.

```
ALTER TABLE my_new_table
ADD CONSTRAINT PK01 PRIMARY KEY (account_id)
```

Dropping a primary key is simply a matter of, once again, altering the table and using the drop keyword in conjunction with the name of the key. The following example shows how the PK we just created would be removed.

```
ALTER TABLE my_new_table
DROP CONSTRAINT PK01
```

If a primary key has a foreign key relationship, you will not be able to drop it until the foreign key is dropped.

Foreign Keys

Foreign Keys are indexes that are created on the second, or foreign, table. A foreign key is "foreign" to the primary table. It acts as a point of connection for the primary table. It is what allows a relationship to the foreign table to exist. Foreign keys facilitate the relationship between the two tables and allow for certain referential integrity constraints to exist and to be enforced. When a foreign key is created, its columns are matched to columns in the primary key of the primary relationship. This allows the two tables to "talk" to each other when data is added, changed, or deleted.

Once defined, a foreign key will require that the values for columns defined in the foreign key be present and match their counterparts in the primary key when data is added or changed. This is a constraint that assures that the data in the foreign table matches up to the data in the primary table. Foreign keys also allow you to define referential integrity rules when they are created. For example, when a record is deleted from the primary table, the delete operation can be cascaded down to the foreign table so that associated rows in the foreign table are also deleted. This can also be done for updates. The RI rules supported varies from one database manufacturer to another. Here are some common ones:

- **CASCADE DELETES**—Forces deletion of foreign table rows based on deletion of primary table rows
- **CASCADE UPDATES**—Forces columns in the foreign key to automatically be updated when their referenced columns in the primary key are changed.
- **NO ACTION**—Does not cascade for updates or deletes

Creation of a foreign key is similar to creating any other constraint. You use the ALTER TABLE DDL command and specify the various aspects of the foreign key. To create the FK it necessary that the primary key already exists, and you must define references to all primary key columns. You do not, however, have to define the RI rules. The following example creates a foreign key that requires matching on the account_id column to the tb_account table (PK) and cascades deletes but not updates.

```
ALTER TABLE tb_order ADD CONSTRAINT FK01
    FOREIGN KEY (account_id)
    REFERENCES my_new_table (account_id)
    ON UPDATE NO ACTION ON DELETE CASCADE
```

Dropping a foreign key is the same as dropping a primary key. You simply use the DROP command. The following drops the FK that we just created.

```
ALTER TABLE my_new_table
DROP CONSTRAINT FK01
```

Chapter 10:
Database Views

All items in a database are usually referred to as "objects." A table is an object and so is an index. Most modern databases support the SQL specification for an object type known as a "View." This type of object provides some features that make using the database easier. Database views provide four primary benefits. They are:

- The ability to alias the names of tables and columns to make them friendlier to the users.

- The ability to pre-define expressions masking their complexity from the users.

- The ability to pre-define table joins making it unnecessary for the database users to understand complex join syntax.

- The ability to create a more complex security model by allowing access to certain views of data without exposing all of the columns in the underlying tables.

What is a View?

A database view is, as its name implies, a way of looking at table data from one or more tables. A database view may or may not show the table structure in the same way that the table does. A database view may also incorporate multiple tables and predefine the joins between them. At its heart a database view is nothing more than a SELECT statement with a name. Think of it as a macro or pre-programmed SQL SELECT statement that you can use over and over. Because it's an object in the database, it is available for use to those who have rights to it all of the time. However, a database view does not store data. It is merely a reference point to the tables in its SELECT statement. Some manufacturers have enhanced the SQL specification to create what are known as materialized views which do store data and require periodic updating. However, the ANSI SQL specifications for a database view do not encompass this functionality.

A Simple Database View

Database views must be created. They are not part of a database by default. They must be "defined" in a manner similar to the way tables are defined. The big difference is that a SELECT statement, not column definitions, will represent the "guts" of a database view. To create a database view, you use the CREATE VIEW command. The syntax to create a database view is as follows:

```
CREATE VIEW ViewName
    (
        SELECT...
    )
```

A view can not have an ORDER BY clause associated with its definition. This is because a view will be used, as though it were a table, in a separate SELECT statement that may have an ORDER BY clause. In the example below a view is created that shows all orders with the corresponding account names next to the order information. It also limits the number of columns exposed by the orders table and sums up the order items to create an order total.

```
CREATE VIEW order_information AS
(
    SELECT
        tb_account.organization_name,
        tb_order.order_id,
        tb_order.date_placed,
        SUM(tb_product.unit_price) AS order_amount
    FROM
        tb_account INNER JOIN tb_order
    ON
        tb_account.account_id = tb_order.account_id
    INNER JOIN
        tb_order_item
    ON
        tb_order_item.order_id = tb_order.order_id
    INNER JOIN
        tb_product
    ON
        tb_product.product_id = tb_order_item.product_id
    GROUP BY
        tb_account.organization_name,
        tb_order.order_id,
        tb_order.date_placed
)
```

If a database view with the same name already exists, the CREATE statement will fail. For this reason you will want to consider dropping the view if it exists first. To do this, simply execute a statement similar to the following, but with your view's name:

```
DROP VIEW order_information
```

Using Views in SELECT Statements

Using a database view is the same as using a database table. Both provide results in the form of columns and rows. To use a database view, you simply need to know the name of the view and have access rights to SELECT against it. In the example below a SELECT statement is executed against a database view.

```
SELECT
    *
FROM
    order_information
ORDER BY
    organization_name, order_id
```

The results would look similar to the follow:

```
organization_name      order_id date_placed         order_amount
-----------------------------------------------------------------
AA Advertising          1730     11/2/2001 1:54:45   856.258
AA Advertising          1795     2/12/2001 11:27:50  21.19
AAA Daniels Antiques    757      8/11/2002 4:20:00   812.279
Acturial Enterprises    596      3/29/2002 10:46:20  296.959
Acturial Enterprises    1049     9/7/2003 11:33:17   1072.63
```

Chapter 11:
Stored Procedures

Stored Procedures provide a means for you to create complex SQL statements and then re-use them. They differ from database views which only support SELECT statement syntax. Stored procedures can include more complex elements of the SQL language. In recent years stored procedures have become a more popular way of manipulating data in databases and seem to be eclipsing database views as a mechanism for storing SQL syntax for reuse.

What is a Stored Procedure?

Stored procedures are objects in a database that allow you to perform a variety of complex and advanced operations. You can think of them as similar to database views, macros, or scripts. Stored procedures can return data, but they can also manipulate data, data structures, and database security. This means that DDL, DML, and DCL statements can be used in Stored Procedures. There are three primary characteristics of stored procedures:

- Store Procedures like Database Views are objects in the database that encapsulate SQL syntax and make it re-usable. Because they can do more than simply return rows stored procedures are sometimes scheduled in job schedulers to perform regular tasks.

- Stored procedures may include complex SQL syntax including syntax that modifies data, data structures and data access.

- Stored procedures are, in some cases, partially compiled making them execute faster on the database server.

A Simple Stored Procedure

Stored procedures can return a result set or operate on data and data structures. To create a stored procedure, you use the CREATE command in a manner similar to creating database tables and views. If a stored procedure with the same name already exists, the CREATE statement will fail. For this reason you will want to consider dropping the stored procedure if it exists first. To do this, simply execute a statement similar to the following, but with your procedure's name:

```
DROP PROCEDURE order_information
```

In the example below, we will create a stored procedure that retrieves data from several tables to create the same order information that the database view returned in an earlier chapter.

```
CREATE PROCEDURE order_information AS
   (
      SELECT
         tb_account.organization_name,
         tb_order.order_id,
         tb_order.date_placed,
         SUM(tb_product.unit_price) AS order_amount
      FROM
      tb_account INNER JOIN tb_order
      ON
         tb_account.account_id = tb_order.account_id
      INNER JOIN
         tb_order_item
      ON
         tb_order_item.order_id = tb_order.order_id
      INNER JOIN
         tb_product
      ON
         tb_product.product_id = tb_order_item.product_id
      GROUP BY
         tb_account.organization_name,
         tb_order.order_id,
         tb_order.date_placed
   )
```

One of the differences between stored procedures and database views is the way in which they are used. A database view simply appears as a table and is used in the same way as a table. A stored procedure must be executed. To make this stored procedure execute, we use the EXEC command with the procedure name as follows:

```
EXEC PROCEDURE order_information
```

Some database systems will execute a stored procedure by simply calling its name as a SQL command.

Parameters in Stored Procedures

Creating a Stored Procedure with Parameters

Stored Procedures differ from database views in several ways. One significant difference is that Stored Procedures may include parameters that allow dynamic information to be passed into the Stored Procedure which then can alter what it does or what records it returns. In the following example, a CREATE statement is used to create a new stored procedure. It includes a parameter called "@region" which is declared with a variable length character data type. The parameter is then used to control which rows are returned. Note its use in the WHERE clause.

```
CREATE PROCEDURE order_information @region VARCHAR(20) AS
(
    SELECT
        tb_account.organization_name,
        tb_order.order_id,
        tb_order.date_placed,
    SUM(tb_product.unit_price) AS order_amount
    FROM
        tb_account INNER JOIN tb_order
    ON
        tb_account.account_id = tb_order.account_id
    INNER JOIN
        tb_order_item
    ON
        tb_order_item.order_id = tb_order.order_id
    INNER JOIN
        tb_product
    ON
        tb_product.product_id = tb_order_item.product_id
    WHERE
        tb_account.region = @region
    GROUP BY
        tb_account.organization_name,
        tb_order.order_id,
        tb_order.date_placed
)
```

Using a Stored Procedure with Parameters

To use this procedure, call it with the parameter value passed via the EXEC command in SQL. The parameter is passed with or without the parameter name. If there were more than one parameter, then the use of the parameter names would be important or the values for each parameter would have to be passed in the order in which the parameters are declared in the Stored Procedure. Parameters are separated by commas in the CREATE command and when calling the procedure with the EXEC command. Here's an example of how a multi parameter procedure would be called:

```
EXEC sp_order_information @region='WI', @country='US'
```

Chapter 12:
SQL Syntax Quick Reference

This chapter provides a quick reference to SQL syntax use. It's provided to prevent you from having to browse entire topics to find syntax examples. The examples in this chapter offer generic syntax and examples to help you find your way through the use of various SQL commands. It is organized by topic. Keep in mind that items that appear in square brackets [ ] are optional.

Simple SELECT Statements

```
SELECT
    [DISTINCT] [*] ColumnName, ColumnName...
FROM
    TableName
ORDER BY
    TableName.ColumnName [Asc, Desc]
```

Will return only the three columns identified:

```
SELECT
    DISTINCT organization_name, phone, city
FROM
    tb_account
ORDER BY
    tb_account.organization_name Asc
```

Will return all columns:

```
SELECT
    *
FROM
    tb_account
ORDER BY
    tb_account.organization_name Asc
```

SELECT Statements (basic WHERE)

```
SELECT
   [DISTINCT] [*] ColumnName, ColumnName...
FROM
   TableName
WHERE
   TableName.Columns [<,>,=,<=,>=] ConstantValue
ORDER BY
   TableName.ColumnName [Asc, Desc]
```

Where account_id is greater than or equal to 100:

```
SELECT
   DISTINCT organization_name, phone, city
FROM
   tb_account
WHERE
   tb_account.account_id >= 100
ORDER BY
   tb_account.organization_name Asc
```

SELECT Statements (advanced WHERE)

```
SELECT
   [DISTINCT] [*] ColumnName, ColumnName...
FROM
   TableName
ORDER BY
   TableName.ColumnName [Asc, Desc]
WHERE
   TableName.Columns [NOT] LIKE '[%]ConstantValue[%]'
[AND|OR]
   TableName.Columns [NOT] LIKE '[%]ConstantValue[%]'
```

Where organization name begins with "O" but doesn't begin with "Oh"

```
SELECT
   DISTINCT organization_name, phone, city
FROM
   tb_account
WHERE
   tb_account.organization_name LIKE 'O%'
AND
   tb_account.organization_name NOT LIKE 'Oh%'
ORDER BY
   tb_account.organization_name Asc
```

Where organization name contains the word "repair" but does not contain the words "New York":

```
SELECT
   DISTINCT organization_name, phone, city
FROM
   tb_account
WHERE
   tb_account.organization_name LIKE '%repair%'
AND
   tb_account.organization_name NOT LIKE '%New York%'
ORDER BY
   tb_account.organization_name Asc
```

Sub-Queries

```
SELECT
    [DISTINCT] [*] ColumnName, ColumnName...
FROM
    TableName1
WHERE
    ConstantValue [NOT] IN
    (
        SELECT
            [DISTINCT] ColumnName
        FROM
            TableName2
        WHERE
            tb_TableName2.ColumnName = tb_
TableName1.ColumnName
    ...
    )
```

Matches order records to accounts not in "CA":

```
SELECT
    *
FROM
    tb_order
WHERE
    'CA' NOT IN
    (
        SELECT
            region
        FROM
            tb_account
        WHERE
            tb_order.account_id = tb_account.account_id
        AND
            Organization_name LIKE '%services%'
    )
```

Joins (Inner & Outer)

Inner Joins require a match on both tables in order for data from either table to be included. An outer join will always include all data from one table (LEFT or RIGHT) and only the matching data from the other table.

SQL3 Syntax

```
SELECT
    [DISTINCT] [*] ColumnName, ColumnName...
FROM
    TableName1 [INNER|LEFT OUTER|RIGHT OUTER] JOIN
TableName2
ON
    TableName1.ColumnName [=,>,<,<=,>=] TableName2.ColumnN
ame [INNER|LEFT OUTER|RIGHT OUTER] JOIN TableName3
ON
    TableName.ColumnName [=,>,<,<=,>=]
TableName3.ColumnName
WHERE
    ...
```

SQL2 Syntax

```
SELECT
    [DISTINCT] [*] ColumnName, ColumnName...
FROM
    TableName1, TableName2
WHERE
    TableName1.ColumnName [=,*=,=*] TableName2.ColumnName
```

In SQL2 = means INNER, *= means LEFT OUTER, =* means RIGHT OUTER

This example joins three tables, the first two with a left outer join and the third with an inner join.

```
SELECT
    DISTINCT organization_name, phone_1, city, tb_
order.order_id,
    date_placed, product_id, unit_sale_amount
FROM
    tb_account LEFT OUTER JOIN tb_order
ON
    Tb_account.account_id = tb_order.account_id
INNER JOIN tb_order_item
ON
    tb_order.order_id = tb_order_item.order_id
```

Joins (Cross)

A Cross Join produces what is known as a Cartesian product. This is every possible combination of data from both sides of the join. A large number of rows may be returned because the number of rows in the second table are multiplied by the number of rows in the first table.

SQL 3 Cross Join Syntax

```
SELECT
    ColumnName, ColumnName...
FROM
    TableName CROSS JOIN TableName
```

SQL2 Cross Join Syntax

```
SELECT
    ColumnName, ColumnName...
FROM
    TableName, TableName
```

A two table cross join

```
SELECT
    *
FROM
    tb_account CROSS JOIN tb_order
```

Joins (Full Outer)

A Full Outer join will include all of the unmatched rows from both the left and right tables.

SQL3 Syntax

```
SELECT
    [DISTINCT] [*] ColumnName, ColumnName...
FROM
    TableName1 FULL OUTER JOIN TableName2
ON
    TableName1.ColumnName [=,>,<,<=,>=]
TableName2.ColumnName
WHERE
    . . .
```

SQL2 Syntax

```
SELECT
    [DISTINCT] [*] ColumnName, ColumnName...
FROM
    TableName1, TableName2
ON
    TableName1.ColumnName *=* TableName2.ColumnName
WHERE
    . . .
```

In the following example, all records from both tables that fail to match the other table will be returned:

```
SELECT
    *
FROM
    tb_account FULL OUTER JOIN tb_order
ON
    tb_account.account_id = tb_order.account_id
```

Joins (Multiple Tables)

SQL3 Syntax

```
SELECT
   ColumnName, ColumnName...
FROM
   Table1Name1 INNER JOIN TableName2
ON
   Table1.ColumnName = Table2.ColumnName
INNER JOIN
   TableName3
ON
   Table2.ColumnName = Table3.ColumnName
AND
   Table1.ColumnName = Table2.ColumnName
```

SQL2 Syntax

```
SELECT
   ColumnName, ColumnName...
FROM
   Table1Name1, TableName2, TableName3
WHERE
   Table1.ColumnName = Table2.ColumnName
AND
   Table3.ColumnName = Table2.ColumnName
```

A three table join example combining LEFT OUTER with INNER:

```
SELECT
   tb_account.city, tb_account.region,
   tb_account.organization_name,
   tb_order.order_id, tb_order.date_placed
FROM
   tb_account LEFT OUTER JOIN tb_prospect
ON
   tb_account.region = tb_prospect.state
AND
   tb_account.city = tb_prospect.city
INNER JOIN
   tb_order
ON
   tb_account.account_id = tb_order.account_id
```

Joins (UNION)

Column names and data types must match for both SELECT statements:

```
SELECT
   [DISTINCT] [*] ColumnName, ColumnName...
FROM
   TableName
WHERE
   ...

UNION

SELECT
   [DISTINCT] [*] ColumnName, ColumnName...
FROM
   TableName
WHERE
   ...
```

Combines account and prospect rows (two separate tables) into a single set of rows:

```
SELECT
   organization_name, city, region, 'Account' as type
FROM
   tb_account

UNION

SELECT
   company_name as organization_name,
   city, state as region, 'Prospect' as type
FROM
   tb_prospect
```

Deriving Data (String Values)

```
SELECT
   [DISTINCT] [*] ColumnName, ColumnName...

RTRIM(ColumnName) + ' ' + LTRIM(ColumnName) AS Contact,
LEFT(ColumnName, 3) + '-' + RIGHT(LEFT(ColumnName, 6),
3) + '-' + RIGHT(ColumnName, 4) AS Name

FROM
   TableName
WHERE
...
```

Assembles first and last contact names with a space between them. Removes leading and trailing spaces (LTRIM, RTRIM), parses phone number and adds dashes (LEFT, RIGHT):

```
SELECT
   organization_name,

RTRIM(tb_account_contact.first_name) + ' ' + LTRIM(tb_
account_contact.last_name) AS Contact,

LEFT(phone, 3) + '-' + RIGHT(LEFT(phone, 6), 3) + '-' +
RIGHT(phone, 4) AS Phone

FROM
   tb_account INNER JOIN tb_account_contact
```

Deriving Data (Math Operations)

```
SELECT
    [DISTINCT] [*] ColumnName, ColumnName...
    ((ColumnName [+,-,*,/] ColumnName)  AS Name
FROM
    TableName
```

An example that calculates a profit percentage

```
SELECT
    product_name, unit_cost, unit_price,
    ((unit_price - unit_cost) / unit_price) * 100 AS
profit_percent
FROM
    tb_product
```

Deriving Data (Date/Time Operations)

```
SELECT
    [DISTINCT] [*] ColumnName, ColumnName...
    ColumnName + 1 AS follow_up_date
FROM
    TableName
```

An example that adds one day to a date/time column:

```
SELECT
    order_id,
    date_placed,
    date_placed + 1 AS follow_up_date
FROM
    tb_order
```

Summarizing Data (SUM, COUNT, AVG, MAX, MIN)

```
SELECT
    [DISTINCT] [*] ColumnName, ColumnName...
    [SUM|COUNT|AVG|MAX|MIN] (ColumnName)
FROM
    TableName
```

This returns a grand total on the unit_price column. The results will be a single column and single row with the amount.

```
SELECT
    SUM(unit_price) AS total_price_all_orders
FROM
    tb_account INNER JOIN tb_order
ON
    tb_account.account_id = tb_order.account_id
INNER JOIN
    tb_order_item
ON
    tb_order_item.order_id = tb_order.order_id
INNER JOIN
    tb_product
ON
    tb_product.product_id = tb_order_item.product_id
```

Summarizing Data (Grouping & Subtotaling)

```
SELECT
   [DISTINCT] [*] ColumnName, ColumnName...
   [SUM|COUNT|AVG](ColumnName)
FROM
   TableName
GROUP BY
   [*] ColumnName, ColumnName...
HAVING
   [SUM|COUNT|AVG](ColumnName) [>,<,=,<=,>=] Value
```

This returns a sub-total on unit_price for each order that has a sub-total that is greater than 100 and only for orders in California

```
SELECT
   tb_order.order_id,
   tb_order.date_placed AS order_date,
   SUM(unit_price) AS order_amount
FROM
   tb_account INNER JOIN tb_order
ON
   tb_account.account_id = tb_order.account_id
INNER JOIN
   tb_order_item
ON
   tb_order_item.order_id = tb_order.order_id
INNER JOIN
   tb_product
ON
   tb_product.product_id = tb_order_item.product_id
WHERE
   tb_account.region = 'CA'
GROUP BY
   tb_order.order_id,
   tb_order.date_placed
```

INSERT

```
INSERT [INTO] TableName
    (ColumnName, ColumnName...)
VALUES
    (Value1, Value2...)
```

The following SQL statement adds a new customer to the Customers table.

```
INSERT INTO
    tb_account
    (account_id, organization_name, street_1, city,
region, country)
VALUES
    (999999, 'Test Organization Name', '123 Street', 'Any
City', 'CA', 'US')
```

Tip: If you do not set a value for a column that does not allow NULL, then the statement will fail.

UPDATE

```
UPDATE TableName SET
   ColumnName = Value,
   ColumnName = Value,
WHERE
   . . .
```

Be very careful issuing UPDATE statements. If the WHERE clause information is not provided then all rows in the table will be updated.

```
UPDATE
   tb_account
SET
   account_id = 888888,
   organization_name = 'My New Organization Name',
   street_1 = '345 Street'
WHERE
   account_id = 999999
```

It's a good idea to use the WHERE clause criteria in a SELECT statement before you attempt to update the rows.

DELETE

DELETE Statement Syntax

```
DELETE FROM
    TableName
WHERE
    ...

DELETE FROM
    tb_account
WHERE
    account_id = 888888
```

If you left off the WHERE clause, all rows would be deleted from the table.

Creating & Changing Table Structure (CREATE, ALTER)

```
CREATE TABLE TableName
  (
  Col1 DataType [NULL|NOT NULL] [DEFAULT default_value],
  Col2 DataType [NULL|NOT NULL] [DEFAULT default_value],
  Col3 DataType [NULL|NOT NULL] [DEFAULT default_value]
  )
```

Common SQL Column Data Types:

- **CHAR: TEXT or STRING** (alphanumeric characters in fixed length)
- **VARCHAR:** (like Char, but variable length)
- **INT: INTEGER** (whole numbers only)
- **CURRENCY or MONEY** (floating point numbers with 4 decimal places)
- **DOUBLE: or FLOAT** (floating point number with X decimal places)
- **DATETIME:** (combination of date & time – will hold just date)
- **BIT: BOOLEAN or BIT** (a true/false value)

Altering an existing table's structure:

```
ALTER TABLE my_new_table
ADD phone VARCHAR(20) NOT NULL DEFAULT 'no phone number'

ALTER TABLE my_new_table
DROP COLUMN phone
```

Creating & Droping Relaitionships (Primary & Foreign Keys)

Primary Key (PK) creation

```
ALTER TABLE TableName
ADD CONSTRAINT KeyName PRIMARY KEY (ColumnName,
ColumnName)
```

Example:

```
ALTER TABLE my_new_table
ADD CONSTRAINT PK01 PRIMARY KEY (account_id)
```

Dropping a Primary Key

```
ALTER TABLE TableName
DROP CONSTRAINT KeyName
```

Foreign Key (FK) Creation

```
ALTER TABLE tb_TableName ADD CONSTRAINT FK01
   FOREIGN KEY (ColumnName, ColumnName)
   REFERENCES PK_ableName (ColumnName, ColumnName)
   ON UPDATE [NO ACTION|CASCADE] ON DELETE [NO
ACTION|CASCADE]
```

Example:

```
ALTER TABLE tb_order ADD CONSTRAINT FK01
   FOREIGN KEY (account_id)
   REFERENCES my_new_table (account_id)
   ON UPDATE NO ACTION ON DELETE CASCADE
```

Dropping a Foreign Key

```
ALTER TABLE my_new_table
DROP CONSTRAINT FK01
```

Creating Database Views

Create View Syntax

```
CREATE VIEW ViewName
   (
      SELECT...
   )
```

Example:

```
CREATE VIEW order_information AS
   (
      SELECT
         tb_account.organization_name,
         tb_order.order_id,
         tb_order.date_placed,
         SUM(tb_product.unit_price) AS order_amount
      FROM
         tb_account INNER JOIN tb_order
      ON
         tb_account.account_id = tb_order.account_id
      INNER JOIN
         tb_order_item
      ON
         tb_order_item.order_id = tb_order.order_id
      INNER JOIN
         tb_product
      ON
         tb_product.product_id = tb_order_item.product_id
      GROUP BY
         tb_account.organization_name,
         tb_order.order_id,
         tb_order.date_placed
   )
```

Creating Stored Procedures

Syntax to Create an SP

```
CREATE PROCEDURE order_information AS
   (
      SELECT...
   )
```

Example:

```
CREATE PROCEDURE order_information AS
   (
    SELECT
       tb_account.organization_name,
       tb_order.order_id,
       tb_order.date_placed,
       SUM(tb_product.unit_price) AS order_amount
    FROM
       tb_account INNER JOIN tb_order
    ON
       tb_account.account_id = tb_order.account_id
    INNER JOIN
       tb_order_item
    ON
       tb_order_item.order_id = tb_order.order_id
    INNER JOIN
       tb_product
    ON
       tb_product.product_id = tb_order_item.product_id
    GROUP BY
       tb_account.organization_name,
       tb_order.order_id,
       tb_order.date_placed
   )
```

Glossary

There are a variety of terms used throughout this text that may be unfamiliar to you. This glossary will serve to help you understand these terms and the context in which they might be used. It may be a good idea to review these terms prior to reading other portions of this text.

ActiveX Data Object (ADO) — An implementation of Microsoft's ActiveX technology for the purpose of providing a standard interface to databases drivers based on the OLEDB standard. This is an advancement from the ODBC data connectivity standard for Windows but includes support for ODBC drivers. ADO is recognized as the preferred standard for connecting to database from Windows applications and Windows based web servers.

Clause — A portion of a SQL statement that usually represents a SQL command or reserved word like WHERE or ORDER BY.

Column — The vertical dimension of a table. A column represents a sub category of data within a table. It is best to think of it the same way you would think of a column in a spreadsheet or ledger. Columns are sometimes referred to as "fields."

Database — A structured and formatted collection of information (data) that can be accessed by various software applications. A database is designed in a predetermined way so as to enforce a standard upon the data stored within it. This makes retrieval and integration of the data more efficient and reliable.

Data Control Language (DCL) — A subset of SQL that provides for the creation and management of security and access control to the database. DCL includes commands like GRANT and REVOKE.

Data Definition Language (DDL)—A subset of SQL that facilitates the creation and modification of SQL objects like tables, views, and stored procedures. DDL Includes commands like CREATE and DROP.

Data Management Language (DML)—A subset of SQL that facilitates the retrieval and management of data. DML includes commands like SELECT, UPDATE, INSERT, and DELETE. It provides for the manipulation and retrieval of the data itself, but does not represent that ability to manipulate the data structure (tables, columns, views, etc.).

Foreign Key—an index on a table the relates to another table's Primary Key and is used to facilitate referential integrity.

Index—A duplication of table data that is "ordered" with a pointer back to the main table for quick reference to table rows and for sorting of table data.

ISAM (Indexed Sequential Access Method)—A manner of storing information that uses indexes to facilitate cross referencing of data.

Join—The term used to represent the connecting of two tables together. In some vendor specific versions of SQL, it is also a reserved word. Joins should not be confused with table relationships which are used to enforce referential integrity. Joins may be performed on any columns between two tables with the same data type and facilitate the retrieval of related data from two or more tables.

ODBC (Open DataBase Connectivity)—A standard created by Microsoft that attempts to facilitate seamless access to a variety of databases from a single software application.

OLEDB/ADO—An advanced, native driver access standard created by Microsoft to facilitate access to databases using a more "native" (faster) method.

Owner—A SQL user account that creates SQL objects and controls them.

Primary Key—An index that must have a unique value for every row in the table. It is also used for "referential integrity."

Quoted Identifiers—Characters that are used in SQL syntax to handle object names with spaces in them. For example, if a table is named "Order Details," then the double quotes would force the SQL server to treat both words as a single name. Quoted identifiers may also be other characters including the [square brackets] characters depending the database manufacturer's requirements.

Relationship—A connection between two tables that may be used to enforce referential integrity. Relationships are defined using Data Definition Language (DDL) and are based on Primary and Foreign Keys.

Referential Integrity—The ability of a relational database to maintain consistency between related tables by allowing the definition of relationships. Relationships help to assure that data is maintained in a consistent and meaningful way. While not always implemented, referential integrity gives the database designer the ability to enforce rules on the creation and manipulation of data so that it accurate.

Row—The horizontal dimension of a table. Rows are where the actual data is stored just as they are in a spreadsheet or ledger. A row is comprised of all the columns of a table. Rows are sometimes referred to as "records."

Server—A computer system that facilitates access and processing of data to users via "Client" software.

SQL—An acronym for "Structured Query Language" which was developed by IBM Corporation to improve the ease and versatility of accessing and managing databases. SQL—sometimes referred to and pronounced as *sequel*—is an acronym representing the language that has become a multi-vendor standard for communicating with databases.

Stored Procedure—A SQL object that is similar to a view but may contain more than one SQL statement and may accept parameters. Stored proceduress are also partially compiled by the SQL server in some cases.

Syntax—The proper formatting of SQL commands and statements that the corresponding database system will accept as legitimate. SQL has several different syntactical variations because it has evolved over time and improved to become more usable and more powerful.

Table—A component of a database that acts as a category for storing a certain topic of data. Tables are best thought of as virtual spreadsheets or ledgers that contain data in a formatted and structured manner. A database will usually have many tables within it, and there will usually be a standard for relating data from one table to another. This is foundation of the Relational Database Management System (RDBMS).

Trigger—A SQL feature that allows you to force certain SQL syntax to execute based on events that occur when data is updated or deleted. Trigger capabilities are vendor specific in most cases.

View—A SQL object that resembles a table but is actually a SQL statement that is retained by the SQL server for re-use.

Bibliography

The Practical SQL Handbook, 3rd Edition: Using Structured Query Language by Judith S. Bowman, Sandra L. Emerson, Marcy Darnovsky (1996, Addison-Wesley)

LAN Times Guide to SQL by James R. Groff, Paul N. Weinberg (1994, Osborne/McGraw-Hill)

Microsoft SQL Server Books On-Line by Microsoft (2000, Microsoft Corporation)

SQL from the Ground Up by Mary Pyefinch (1999, Osborne/McGraw-Hill)

Index

CPSIA information can be obtained at www.ICGtesting.com
Printed in the USA
LVOW051533160612

286417LV00001BA/98/A